MAKING SUGAR MODELS

DEDICATION

To my wonderfully supportive husband Paul
and to my family and friends. Without them
behind me I would not be reaching for the stars.

My love and thanks to you, the reader. I
wouldn't be here without you.

First published in January 2020 by B. Dutton
Publishing Limited, The Packhouse, Blackmoor
Estate, Blackmoor, Liss, Hampshire, GU33 6BS, UK.

Copyright: B. Dutton Publishing 2020

ISBN-13: 978-1-905113-61-3

Printed and bound in Turkey by Imago Publishing Limited.

Publisher: Beverley Dutton

Editor-in-Chief: Adele Duthie

Creative Director: Sarah Ryan

Photography: Alister Thorpe

Disclaimer

The Authors and Publisher have made every effort to ensure
that the contents of this book, if followed carefully, will not
cause harm or injury or pose any danger. Please note that
some inedible items, such as floral wires, have been used
in the projects in this book. All such inedible items must
be removed from a cake before it is eaten. Similarly, any
equipment and substances not approved for contact with
food, such as non-toxic glue, must not come into contact
with anything that is to be eaten. Neither the Authors nor the
Publisher can be held responsible for errors or omissions and
cannot accept liability for injury, damage or loss to persons
or property, however it may arise, as a result of acting upon
guidelines and information printed in this book.

MAKING SUGAR MODELS

INTRODUCTION

To say I am excited to share this with you is an understatement! This is my first book and it's a dream come true for me. It's the kind of book I wish I had when I started baking and decorating cakes: a bible of cake decoration that will end up covered in cake batter, food colouring and sticky fingerprints as you flick through the pages whilst you work.

My passion is sugar modelling so I wanted the focus to be on just that. There are over 50 individual characters to get stuck into including my personal favourites, the baby jungle animals. I've tried to include as much of my knowledge as possible and I hope that it proves to be a valuable resource for beginners and more advanced students.

Of course, I couldn't leave you without a cake to adorn so, at the end of each character section, there are instructions on how to decorate a complementary cake too. I've designed a range of cakes for every occasion, all with step-by-step instructions, so that you can have fun recreating them throughout the year. I've also included some hints and tips I've picked up over the years and ideas for customising the designs, which you will hopefully find useful.

Once you've got the hang of the techniques, all the cakes and models can be adapted to suit your needs and you should feel free to combine and change the designs as you see fit. After all, these cakes are for you, and they should be exactly what you want them to be.

I really hope this book gives you the confidence to create your own characters. I would love to hear from you so please get in touch and send me your cake photos or any questions you may have. Enjoy!

CONTENTS

94

SPOOKY CHARACTERS

102

SANTA'S LITTLE HELPERS

114

PESKY MICE

124

BUNCH OF BUNNIES

132

WOODLAND CRITTERS

142

BABY ANIMALS

154

PRIDE OF LIONS

162

GARDEN GANG

170

PREHISTORIC PALS

ESSENTIAL EDIBLES AND EQUIPMENT

When I started cake decorating, I was determined not to purchase too many tools. Here's a list of the essential items that you'll need to create the cakes in this book.

NON-STICK BOARD

For modelling, an A4 or similar size, board is perfect. Pop a non-slip mat underneath it to make sure the board stays in place as you work.

CAKE SMOOTHERS

These solid paddles are great for smoothing sugarpaste over cakes and boards. You can also use them to roll even sausage shapes (see page 17).

FLEXI SMOOTHERS

Unlike standard smoothers, these are flexible and clear so you can see what you're doing as you work. They're designed for creating sharp edges on sugarpaste-covered cakes and are also great for smoothing out any tiny imperfections.

NON-STICK ROLLING PIN

I recommend a 23cm (9") pin for modelling work and a minimum 38cm (15") pin for covering cakes.

CORNFLOUR

When modelling, it's best to dust surfaces with cornflour rather than icing sugar as it's a lot finer and smoother. Wrap 3tbsp of cornflour in a sheet of muslin cloth to create a powder puff which will transfer the perfect amount of dust to your board.

DRUMS AND BOARDS

Use these as a base for all of your cakes, with thicker cake drums supporting the whole cake and thinner cake boards underneath each cake tier.

CAKE DOWELS

These plastic rods are used to support the tiers of a stacked cake (see page 31). They're also used as internal supports for larger sugar models.

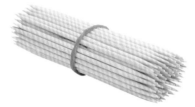

COCKTAIL STICKS

These are a very handy, great value item to have in your tool kit. They're useful for supporting models, especially their heads, and for adding paste colours to sugarpaste.

WOODEN BARBECUE SKEWERS

Like a cocktail stick, but bigger. I rely on these to form the base supports for all of my models.

FLORAL WIRES

Wires aren't just for sugar flowers, they're also great for supporting curved shapes that a wooden skewer wouldn't accommodate.

SMALL SCISSORS

In some instances, using a knife might leave a cut mark on your work. This is when small scissors come in handy. You don't need to put pressure on any other parts of the model, just snip the necessary piece of paste away.

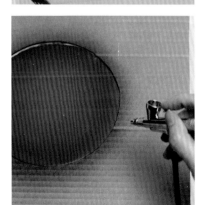

AIRBRUSH

Airbrushes are surprisingly easy to use but I think most people are too scared to try them out. I had mine for a year before I dared to try using it. Looking back, I wish I had just jumped right in because it is an amazing piece of kit for adding shading and depth of colour (see page 12).

GETTING TO KNOW PASTES

Spot the difference! Fondant, sugarpaste, modelling paste, gum paste, flower paste, petal paste, Mexican paste – sugar has a lot of names! Here's a quick introduction to the properties of each one and when to use them.

losing their shape. They are useful for all characters, including animals and people, as you can add fine details like fur and facial expressions.

Looking to cover a cake? You'll need some **sugarpaste**, also known as ready-to-roll icing and fondant (but not pouring fondant*). It comes at various price points, from supermarket own brands to high-end versions. Many brands also sell pre-coloured sugarpaste, in addition to white, which can save you some time. Find out how to cover a cake with sugarpaste on page 28. You can also use royal icing to cover a cake but this is a wet icing you'd apply with a palette knife rather than a roll-out paste.

Modelling? Try **modelling paste**, gum paste or Mexican paste. These pastes are stretchier, stronger and more pliable than sugarpaste. This added magic allows you to create models that will set without sinking or

You can also knead small amounts of **CMC** (Tylo Powder) or gum tragacanth into sugarpaste to make your own modelling paste. This is useful for simple shapes that don't need to support weight, or for cake-side decorations like hills or wooden planks. Making this treated sugarpaste is cheaper than buying readymade modelling paste, however, it doesn't have the strength to hold its shape when creating detailed models. If you need a model to set quickly, you can add CMC to readymade modelling paste to create a fast-drying paste.

Making flowers or fine details? You'll want **Sugar Florist Paste (SFP)**, flower paste or petal paste. This paste is incredibly strong and stretchy and can be rolled really fine. It dries firmer than most modelling pastes and is useful for delicate details such as ribbons, bows and eyelashes. It's also great for lettering, particularly when using intricate cutters.

Piping words or patterns? **Royal icing** is the way to go. If you want to pipe simple letters or shapes then the boxes you can pick up in the supermarket are

fine. If you're attempting some more elaborate piping, I'd advise buying a more high-end product or making your own from scratch. I don't often use royal icing in my designs but there are plenty of tutorials online which will help you get the hang of recipes, consistencies and piping techniques.

*In the UK, the icing drizzled over buns, éclairs and French fancies is called fondant icing. This often causes confusion as sugarpaste is called fondant in the USA.

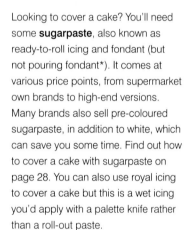

TOP TIP

If you find a model is not holding up using modelling paste alone, try mixing modelling paste 50:50 with flower paste to make a firmer, stronger formula.

EDIBLE GLUE

You can buy edible glue from cake decorating stores or make your own. My homemade version lasts around one week. To increase its shelf life to up to three weeks you can add a small amount of clear alcohol, such as vodka or gin.

YOU WILL NEED

30ml (1fl oz) boiled water

Small glass jar with lid, sterilised

1/8tsp CMC Cellulose Gum

1 Pour boiled water into the sterilised glass jar.

2 Sprinkle the CMC powder over the surface of the water, creating a thin layer.

3 Set the jar aside overnight then stir to combine.

TROUBLESHOOTING

If the glue is too stiff and jelly-like, add more boiled water.

If the glue is too runny, add more CMC.

FOOD COLOURS

As well as working with pre-coloured sugar pastes, there are all sorts of food colours you can use to enhance your designs. Here is a run-down of the different formulas and when it's best to use each one.

PASTE OR GEL COLOURS

When colouring modelling paste, you want to use a product that doesn't alter the consistency by adding or removing moisture. Paste- or gel- based food colours are ideal. They're really simple to use and come in a wide variety of colours. To use them, knead the paste until it's elastic and create a well in the centre. Dip a cocktail stick into the food colour, apply it to the well then fold and knead the paste until the colour is evenly distributed.

TOP TIPS

Aim to colour modelling paste at least one hour before you need to use it. That way, the paste has a chance to cool and return to its original state. Trying to model with too-soft paste can be frustrating as it won't retain its shape as well.

To create a marbled effect, stop folding and kneading before the colour is evenly distributed, leaving trails of more concentrated colour throughout the paste.

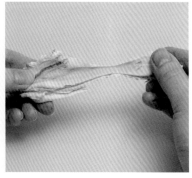
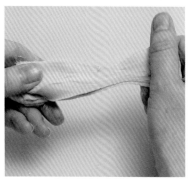

DUST OR POWDER COLOURS

Dust colours are used to add depth and extra detailing to your work. It's best to let your model set before dusting, otherwise you may end up leaving marks from the paintbrush on the smooth surface. I use a contouring brush to add blush to my characters and a wide, fluffy brush to add shading. The brilliant thing about dust colours is that you can mix them with clear alcohol, like vodka or gin, to create an edible paint which can be used to add fine details, and even make up, to your models.

TOP TIP

If you're mixing up a custom dust colour, make up more than you need and keep it in a small, food-safe tub for future use.

AIRBRUSH COLOURS

Airbrush colours are specially formulated with fine particles suspended in liquid, meaning they give even coverage over small or large areas and are nicely buildable. My top tip for using an airbrush would be to only half-fill the cup, that way there's less chance of spillage. I'd also advise starting off cautiously and gradually building up the colour. If you're too nervous to try it straight on a cake, try practising in a colouring book or some paper first.

TOP TIP

Shampoo is really good at removing food colour from your skin.

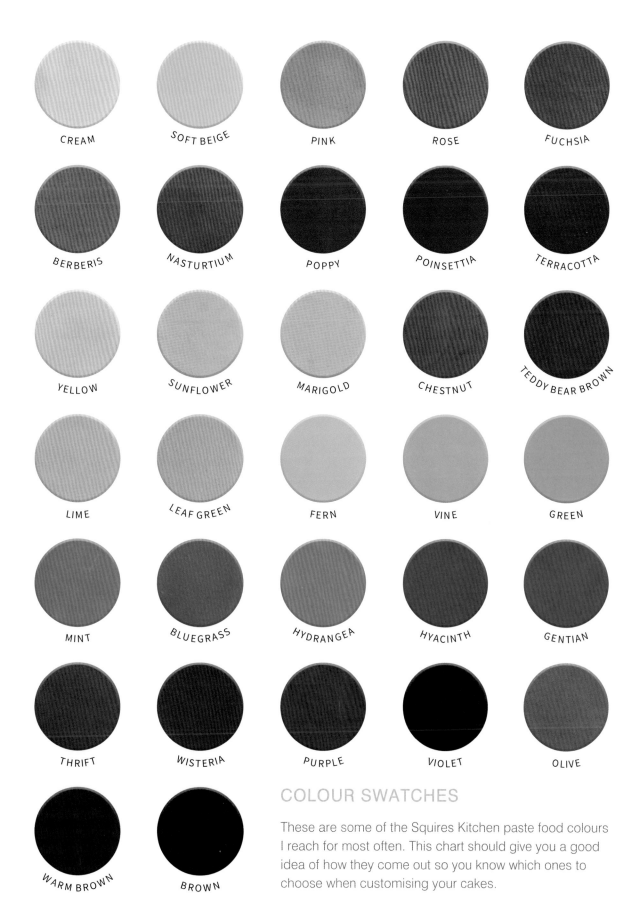

CREAM

SOFT BEIGE

PINK

ROSE

FUCHSIA

BERBERIS

NASTURTIUM

POPPY

POINSETTIA

TERRACOTTA

YELLOW

SUNFLOWER

MARIGOLD

CHESTNUT

TEDDY BEAR BROWN

LIME

LEAF GREEN

FERN

VINE

GREEN

MINT

BLUEGRASS

HYDRANGEA

HYACINTH

GENTIAN

THRIFT

WISTERIA

PURPLE

VIOLET

OLIVE

WARM BROWN

BROWN

COLOUR SWATCHES

These are some of the Squires Kitchen paste food colours I reach for most often. This chart should give you a good idea of how they come out so you know which ones to choose when customising your cakes.

TOP TOOLS

Modelling tools are an essential piece of kit for any sugarcrafter. I have a few absolute favourites that I could not live without, so I've listed them here along with explanations for their usage and ideas on how to use them.

DRESDEN TOOL

The Dresden tool (or petal and leaf shaper) is my number one choice for modelling. Both sides of this dual-ended tool are great for sculpting, defining, blending and creating texture. It's my go-to for almost every job. You can use it to create mouths, make eye sockets, texture hair and fur, draw lines and grooves and blend seams.

BALL TOOL

This is my second favourite tool to use. You'll want to collect a variety of sizes – the more, the better. Pressing lightly with a larger ball will create a shallow well that can be used to create depth on a character's face. If you press harder you can create more defined wells for dimples, eye sockets, ear holes and pupils.

SCRIBING TOOL

Often overlooked, this needle-like tool comes in thick and thin versions and they're both incredibly handy. The thin tool is great for adding fine, defined lines to your sugar models. I use it to create fabric creases, teeth, hair and fur, and to assist in positioning tiny pieces of paste. The thicker needle can be used to create wider lines but I find it most useful for boring holes in cake boards to hold wooden skewers and cake dowels.

BRUSHES

I tend to only use classic artists' paintbrushes for painting; make sure you have a range of sizes and that they're suitable for food contact. To apply dust colours I prefer to use makeup brushes, particularly contour brushes, which have more tightly packed bristles and a wide, flat surface. They're perfect for applying a light, diffused layer of dust colour to create flushed faces and shading.

CRAFT KNIFE

Why have one, when you can have two? I always have two knives with me because, when I work, I find the blades gets sticky fast and it becomes difficult to produce neat cuts. I use the second knife to scrape away the residue from the first blade to ensure I can work quickly and cleanly.

CUTTING WHEEL

This tool is great for cutting out clothing for a model, or cutting a strip. Once paste is rolled out, a craft knife can end up dragging, ripping and stretching the paste. Swap the knife for a cutting wheel or pastry wheel and the cuts will be far smoother. Just make sure you tidy up the edges as the wheel tool will not leave as neat a finish as a sharp knife would.

SILICONE-TIPPED TOOL

These soft-tipped tools are ideal for doing what your hands can't. I use them to blend, move and smooth paste in areas that are too small and delicate to work with my fingers. Look for tools with large, rounded tips to use as mini fingers and small, pointed tips to add soft detailing that a Dresden tool would be too stiff for.

BASIC SHAPES

When you're just starting out, it's helpful to practise creating the core shapes that will be used to build almost everything you'll make. These are all of my most frequently used shapes, along with tips and tricks for how to create them. Once you have these mastered, your sugar modelling will automatically become so much quicker and easier.

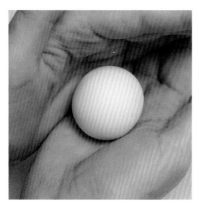

THE BALL

This is as simple as it gets, but it is the most fundamental of all shapes. Every shape should start from a ball, even a cube! The ball ensures you have a nice, smooth shape to start your model, with no cracks or creases. Roll the paste between the palms of your hands to create a smooth, crack-free ball.

THE CONE

This shape can prove difficult for some, whilst others master it with ease. Roll a ball in the palm of your hand. Place the side of your hand halfway along the ball and gently roll back and forth to thin and shape the cone.

THE EGG

This shape is very similar to the cone, just with a rounded end instead of a point at the narrow end. It's perfect for animal bodies and human faces.

TOP TIP

If you're struggling to smooth out the creases and cracks, try rolling the ball in the opposite direction.

The next time you look at a sugar model, try to spot all of the basic shapes that have been used to create it. Breaking it down into its component parts will make it feel so much less daunting.

When I first started cake decorating, I used to sit in front of the TV with a lap tray and a ball of modelling paste. I'd create all sorts of random shapes and the practice helped improve my skills. There's no pressure to create the perfect model; if it doesn't look right, roll it into a ball and start again. Or eat it, because sometimes that helps with frustration!

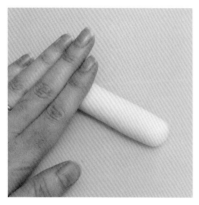 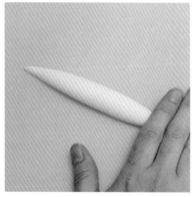 

THE SAUSAGE

Apart from being used to create sugar sausages, this shape has a variety of uses. Roll thin sausages when creating hair or chunkier sausages for arms and legs. Start with a ball then roll it back and forth between your palms or on your work surface to thin and shape the paste. Move your fingers as you work to avoid creating any lumps and bumps.

THE TAPERED SAUSAGE

This is a hybrid of the cone and the sausage. It's useful for hair, eyebrows, arms, legs and tails. Whilst rolling out the sausage, apply more pressure to one side, thinning the end to a point. Some of my tutorials call for both ends to be tapered. To do this, just flip the sausage over and repeat the process at the opposite end.

THE DISC

This shape is perfect for hooves, collars and wheels. Start with a ball then gently press down on the ball to flatten it into a disc. If you want a straight-sided disc, pinch around the edge with your fingers then roll the disc on its narrow side to smooth away any finger marks.

TOP TIP

Use a cake smoother to roll the paste when making sausages and discs for a smooth, even finish.

RECIPES

These are the tried and tested recipes that form the basis of my designs. In both
of the cake recipes the mixture is divided between two tins, allowing the cakes
to rise and cook without developing a dark crust. The cakes should each rise to a
depth of approximately 5cm (2"), creating a nice tall cake when combined.

TOP TIP

You can buy ready-cut parchment
cake tin liners which will help speed
up lining the tins dramatically.

VANILLA SPONGE

This is a classic Victoria sponge recipe. It's light and fluffy and tastes great filled with buttercream and jam.

METHOD

1 Preheat the oven to 160°C (140°C fan/325°F/gas mark 3). Grease and line two cake tins of the same size.

2 Place the margarine in the bowl of a stand mixer and beat until softened. Add the caster sugar and continue to beat for a minute or so until pale and fluffy.

3 Sieve the flour into a bowl. Break the eggs into a measuring jug and beat them lightly with a fork.

4 Turn the mixer down to its lowest speed and add some of the beaten egg, beating until combined. Continue gradually adding egg until the mixture looks to be on the verge of splitting, then add a spoonful of flour. Repeat until all of the egg has been added.

5 Pour in the remaining flour and mix until just combined. Be careful not to over-mix at this stage or you could end up with a dense cake.

6 Add the vanilla extract and mix until combined.

7 Divide the mixture between the two lined cake tins.

8 Place the tins on the lowest shelf in your oven and bake for the time listed in the table, or until the cakes are pulling away from the sides of the tins and a skewer inserted into the centre of each one comes out clean.

9 Remove the cakes from the tins and allow to cool on a wire cooling rack.

ROUND	12.5cm (5")	15cm (6")	18cm (7")	20.5cm (8")	23cm (9")	25.5cm (10")
SQUARE	10cm (4")	12.5cm (5")	15cm (6")	18cm (7")	20.5cm (8")	23cm (9")
Margarine	190g (6¾oz)	250g (8¾oz)	300g (10½oz)	450g (1lb)	550g (1lb 3½oz)	700g (1lb 8¾oz)
Caster Sugar	190g (6¾oz)	250g (8¾oz)	300g (10½oz)	450g (1lb)	550g (1lb 3½oz)	700g (1lb 8¾oz)
Eggs (Medium)	4	5	6	9	11	14
Self-Raising Flour	190g (6¾oz)	250g (8¾oz)	300g (10½oz)	450g (1lb)	550g (1lb 3½oz)	700g (1lb 8¾oz)
Vanilla Extract	2tsp	3tsp	3tsp	4tsp	5tsp	5tsp
Cooking Time	40 minutes	50 minutes	1 hour 10 minutes	1 hour 30 minutes	1 hour 40 minutes	1 hour 50 minutes
PORTIONS	6–8	12–16	18–24	24–30	28–40	35–50

CHOCOLATE SPONGE

This is a light chocolate sponge that's perfect for kids and adults alike. It's great coupled with raspberry jam or try it with vanilla buttercream and cherry jam for a Black Forest gateau feel.

METHOD

1 Preheat the oven to 160°C (140°C fan/325°F/gas mark 3). Grease and line two cake tins of the same size.

2 Pour the cocoa powder into the bowl of a stand mixer and stir in the boiled water to form a paste.

3 Once the paste has cooled, add the margarine and beat until combined. Add the caster sugar and continue to beat for a minute or so until the mixture becomes pale and fluffy.

4 Sieve the flour into a bowl. Break the eggs into a measuring jug and beat them lightly with a fork.

5 Turn the mixer down to its lowest speed and add some of the beaten egg, beating until combined. Continue gradually adding egg until the mixture looks to be on the verge of splitting, then add a spoonful of flour. Repeat until all of the egg has been added.

6 Pour in the remaining flour and mix until just combined. Be careful not to over-mix at this stage or you could end up with a dense cake.

7 Add the vanilla extract and mix until combined.

ROUND	12.5cm (5")	15cm (6")	18cm (7")	20.5cm (8")	23cm (9")	25.5cm (10")
SQUARE	10cm (4")	12.5cm (5")	15cm (6")	18cm (7")	20.5cm (8")	23cm (9")
Cocoa Powder	20g (¾oz)	25g (>¾oz)	30g (1oz)	45g (1½oz)	550g (1lb 3½oz)	700g (1lb 8¾oz)
Boiled Water	40ml (1½fl oz)	50ml (1¾fl oz)	60ml (2fl oz)	90ml (3fl oz)	110ml (3¾fl oz)	140ml (5fl oz)
Margarine	190g (6¾oz)	250g (8¾oz)	300g (10½oz)	450g (1lb)	550g (1lb 3½oz)	700g (1lb 8¾oz)
Caster Sugar	190g (6¾oz)	250g (8¾oz)	300g (10½oz)	450g (1lb)	550g (1lb 3½oz)	700g (1lb 8¾oz)
Eggs (Medium)	4	5	6	9	11	14
Self-Raising Flour	190g (6¾oz)	250g (8¾oz)	300g (10½oz)	450g (1lb)	550g (1lb 3½oz)	700g (1lb 8¾oz)
Vanilla Extract	2tsp	3tsp	3tsp	4tsp	5tsp	5tsp
Cooking Time	40 minutes	50 minutes	1 hour 10 minutes	1 hour 30 minutes	1 hour 40 minutes	1 hour 50 minutes
PORTIONS	6–8	12–16	18–24	24–30	28–40	35–50

8   Divide the mixture between the two lined cake tins.

9   Place the tins on the lowest shelf in your oven and bake for the time listed in the table, or until the cakes are pulling away from the sides of the tins and a skewer inserted into the centre of each one comes out clean.

10 Remove the cakes from the tins and allow to cool on a wire cooling rack.

NOTES ON PORTIONS

If you like a lot of cake per portion, work to the lower figure on the portion guide for each cake.

Bear in mind that these recipes bake particularly tall cakes. Once filled and assembled, a 2.5cm (1") finger potion will yield a slice of cake almost 15cm (6") tall. Even I struggle with that on some days!

VARIATIONS

Add a splash of instant coffee to create a mocha cake or a dash of peppermint extract to create a mint chocolate cake.

VANILLA CUPCAKES

The quantities listed in the table will give you flat cupcakes ideal for topping with discs of sugarpaste and modelled characters. Try adding a little lemon or orange zest in place of the vanilla extract for fruity flavours.

METHOD

1 Pre-heat the oven to 160°C (140°C fan/325°F/gas mark 3). Line a muffin tin with cupcake cases.

2 Place the margarine in the bowl of a stand mixer and beat until softened. Add the caster sugar and continue to beat for a minute or so until pale and fluffy.

3 Sieve the flour into a bowl. Break the eggs into a measuring jug and beat them lightly with a fork.

4 Turn the mixer down to its lowest speed and add some of the beaten egg, beating until combined. Continue gradually adding egg until the mixture looks to be on the verge of splitting, then add a spoonful of flour. Repeat until all of the egg is added.

5 Pour in the remaining flour and mix until just combined. Add the vanilla extract and mix until combined.

6 Use an ice cream scoop to transfer one full scoop of mixture to each cupcake case. Once they are all filled, give the tin a little shake from side to side to distribute the mixture to the sides of the cases.

7 Place the muffin tin on the lowest shelf in your oven and cook until the cupcakes are golden and spring back when gently touched.

8 Remove the cupcakes from the tin and allow to cool on a wire cooling rack.

QUANTITY	6	12	24
Margarine	65g (2¼oz)	135g (4¾oz)	270g (9½oz)
Caster Sugar	65g (2¼oz)	135g (4¾oz)	270g (9½oz)
Eggs (Large)	1	2	4
Self-Raising Flour	65g (2¼oz)	135g (4¾oz)	270g (9½oz)
Vanilla Extract	½tsp	1tsp	2tsp
Cooking Time	20–25 minutes	20–25 minutes	20–25 minutes

VANILLA BUTTERCREAM

The buttercream quantities I've listed here will give you enough to fill and crumb coat your cakes. You can also swap the unsalted butter for the same quantity of margarine to create a lighter buttercream for topping cupcakes.

METHOD

1 Place the butter or margarine in the bowl of a stand mixer fitted with the beater attachment. Starting low, gradually turn the mixer up to its highest speed and beat until softened.

2 Scrape down the sides of the mixing bowl and add the icing sugar. Start beating on a low speed until all of the icing sugar is combined, then beat on a high speed for around four minutes until the buttercream is light, fluffy and pale in colour.

3 Add the boiled water and continue to beat until combined.

4 Add the vanilla extract and beat to combine.

5 The buttercream can be covered with cling film and refrigerated for up to one week. Return to room temperature and re-beat before use.

ROUND	12.5cm (5")	15cm (6")	18cm (7")	20.5cm (8")	23cm (9")	25.5cm (10")
SQUARE	10cm (4")	12.5cm (5")	15cm (6")	18cm (7")	20.5cm (8")	23cm (9")
Unsalted Butter	150g (5¼oz)	200g (7oz)	250g (8¾oz)	350g (12¼)	400g (14oz)	500g (1lb 1¾oz)
Icing Sugar	150g (5¼oz)	400g (14oz)	500g (1lb 1¾oz)	700g (1lb 8¾oz)	800g (1lb 12oz)	1kg (2lb 3¼oz)
Boiled Water	¾tsp	1tsp	1tsp	1½tsp	2tsp	2tsp
Vanilla Extract	1tsp	1tsp	1tsp	2tsp	2tsp	3tsp

TOP TIP

Before turning on the mixer, cover the bowl with a slightly damp tea towel to prevent a mushroom cloud of icing sugar from covering your kitchen.

BASIC TECHNIQUES

Before you get onto the decorating, you have to prepare your cake to be decorated. In this section I show you everything from cutting to covering your cake.

CAKE-MAKING SCHEDULE

Day 1: Bake and crumb coat the cake(s)

Day 2: Cover the cake(s) and drum

Day 3 onwards: Decorate the cake

CONSTRUCTING A CAKE

I like to get my cakes crumb coated as soon as I can after baking, that way the cake stays fresh. I have found that leaving it until the next day sometimes makes the cake a little dry.

1   Measure the height of the baked cake, discounting any doming on top. Divide the figure in half and make marks at this height around the sides of the cake. Use a serrated knife to gently cut into the cake at the marked points to around a 1cm ($^3/_8$") depth. Continue around the cake until you reach the initial cut. Once you're happy that the cut lines up around the side of the cake, gently take the knife deeper, turning the cake as you cut, until the cake is split in half.

2   Use the same technique to level the top of the cake, creating a second layer of sponge the same depth as the first.

3   Repeat steps 1–2 to divide the second cake into two even layers of the same depth, creating a total of four even layers.

4   Spread a thin layer of buttercream over a cake board the same diameter as the cake. Place one of the base layers of sponge on top and gently press down to fix it in place.

5   Pipe or spoon buttercream over the top of the cake layer and use a cranked palette knife to spread it evenly to the edges. Don't worry about being too neat at this stage, just make sure the buttercream is as level as possible. The weight from the cake layer above will flatten any bumps.

6   Spread a thin layer of jam over the bottom of the second sponge layer. Turn the sponge over and place it, jam-side-down, on top of the buttercream-covered layer.

7   Repeat steps 5–6 using the remaining two layers of sponge, topping it with the base of the second cake with the bottom edge uppermost – this will ensure a flat top surface.

8   Refrigerate the assembled cake for 30 minutes before applying the crumb coat.

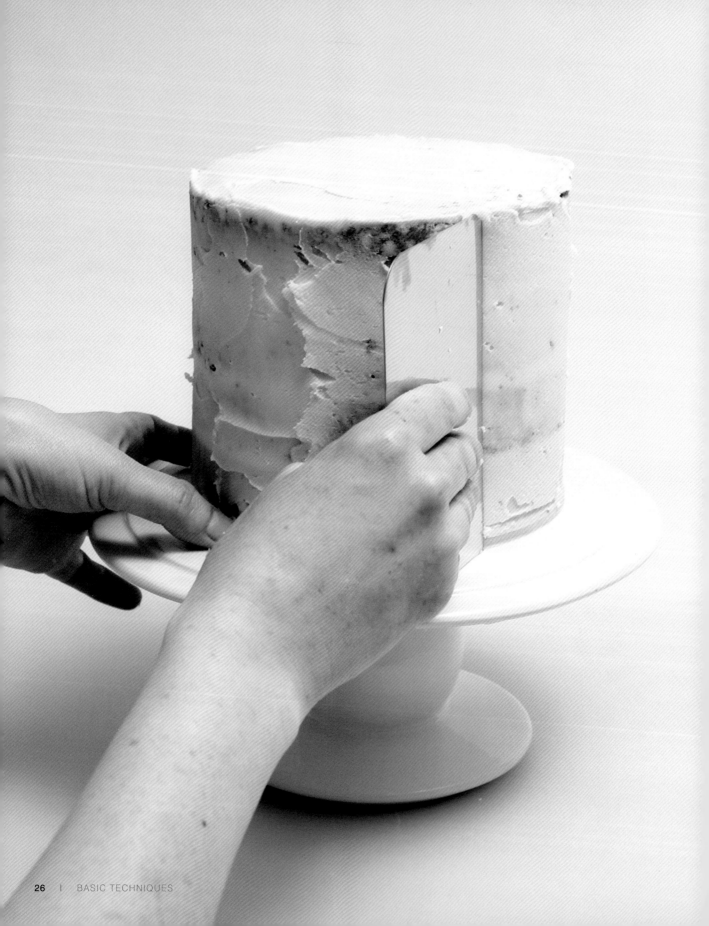

CRUMB COATING A CAKE

Crumb coating is so called as it's the layer of icing that traps the cake crumbs. If you were using buttercream to decorate your cake it would prevent any crumbs from creeping into the outer coats and making it look untidy. However, as we're using sugarpaste in these tutorials, its use here is to bond the sugarpaste to the cake. Because it will be covered, you can be pretty slapdash with the buttercream to start with, as long as the outer coating is smooth and crisp once you've finished.

1 Spread a thick layer of buttercream over the sides of the cake, supporting the cake as you work by gently holding the top. Don't worry about being neat at this stage.

2 Place a side scraper directly on the cake board, keeping its base in contact with the board at all times. This will ensure the scraper stays at a right angle to the cake and you get a

straight edge. Run the scraper around the side of the cake. When it comes to the edge, pull away and remove any excess buttercream before repeating. Continue until the sides are smooth.

3 Spread a thin layer of buttercream over the top of the cake. Pull the scraper across the top of the cake, from the edge inwards, removing excess buttercream until the surface is smooth.

4 Fill in any dents on the top and side of the cake with extra buttercream and repeat the scraping process until the surface is beautifully smooth.

5 Refrigerate the cake for a minimum of four hours. The cooler the cake, the easier it will be to cover and the less chance there is of any bulges appearing in the sugarpaste.

COVERING A CAKE

Honestly, this is the part of cake decorating that I always feel a little bit apprehensive about. And you know what? That's ok! You don't have to love every part of the process. Before you get started covering the cake you need to make sure it has been properly chilled and that you have applied a layer of cooled, boiled water to the surface to make it tacky, but not wet.

1 Knead the sugarpaste until it's soft and pliable. Once ready, the paste shouldn't have any cracks, tears or elephant skin when it is folded.

2 Sprinkle icing sugar over your work surface and place the ball of sugarpaste in the centre.

3 Using a large rolling pin, begin to roll over the paste back and forth, rolling away from and towards your body.

TOP TIP

You may see little bubbles forming in the sugarpaste as you roll. If so, use a scribing tool to prick the bubble and gently press the air out of the hole.

4 Lift the sheet of sugarpaste and rotate it 90 degrees. Repeat step 3 to continue to roll out the paste, creating as even a shape as possible.

TOP TIPS

If you struggle to roll sugarpaste out to an even thickness, try using marzipan spacers. Place the spacers on either side of the sugarpaste and follow steps 3–4 until the rolling pin makes contact with the spacers.

Never flip a sheet of sugarpaste upside down whilst rolling out or you'll end up with icing sugar all over the surface, resulting in a dull and tarnished cake.

5 Repeat steps 3–4 until the sugarpaste is rolled out to a 4mm ($^3/_{16}$") thickness and is of a sufficient size to cover your cake.

TOP TIP

Measure the diameter and depth of your cake. Add together one diameter and two depths to find the size to which you need to roll out the sugarpaste. I always add an extra 10cm (4") to aid covering.

6 Lift the edge of the sheet of sugarpaste and slide your hands underneath, palm-side up. Move your hands to a position where you can support the paste as you lift. Gently lift the paste and take it to the cake. Lower the sugarpaste into position and remove your hands.

7 Working quickly, smooth the sugarpaste over the top of the cake with your hands and gently work it around the edges. This should ensure the sugarpaste does not tear.

8 Use your hands to work your way down the sides of the cake gradually, smoothing the paste and pressing it to the sides of the cake. Redistribute the skirt of sugarpaste to remove pleats.

TOP TIP

Until you are confident at covering a cake, roll the sugarpaste out 10–15cm (4–5") larger than required. It is easier to redistribute the pleats that form if you're working with a larger area of sugarpaste.

9 Trim away the excess sugarpaste with a sharp knife. Use the smoothers to smooth the paste. Flexi smoothers are particularly helpful as you can see and feel the cake as you smooth.

10 Once you're happy with the finish, leave the cake to firm for 24 hours before decorating. If you're especially impatient you can decorate straight away but you run the risk of marking the sugarpaste covering.

SUGGESTED SUGARPASTE QUANTITIES FOR COVERING CAKES

SIZE	Round	Square
10cm (4")	600g (1lb 5¼oz)	700g (1lb 8¾oz)
12.5cm (5")	700g (1lb 8¾oz)	800g (1lb 12oz)
15cm (6")	800g (1lb 12oz)	900g (2lb)
18cm (7")	900g (2lb)	1kg (2lb 3¼oz)
20.5cm (8")	1kg (2lb 3¼oz)	1.1kg (2lb 6¾oz)
23cm (9")	1.1kg (2lb 6¾oz)	1.3kg (2lb 13¾oz)
25.5cm (10")	1.3kg (2lb 13¾oz)	1.5kg (3lb 5oz)

COVERING A DRUM

Also known as a board, a thick cake drum covered with sugarpaste is a great way to construct, transport and display your cake. The covering is a simple job which should be completed at least 24 hours before you are ready to assemble the cake, that way you won't leave dents in the sugarpaste as you are working.

1 Brush a layer of cooled, boiled water over the surface of the cake drum.

2 Repeat steps 1–4 from the Covering a Cake instructions on page 28, this time rolling out the sugarpaste to a 5mm (¼") thickness.

3 Lift the sugarpaste and lay it over the cake drum. Use a cake smoother to smooth the surface of the sugarpaste.

4 Lift the drum, holding it from beneath with one hand. With the other hand, run a sharp knife around the edge of the drum, trimming away the excess sugarpaste from around the edge. Be sure to clean the knife thoroughly, removing any sugarpaste, to ensure a smooth cut.

5 Give the sugarpaste another smooth then run your fingers around the edge to remove any jagged edges.

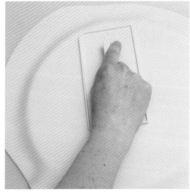

STACKING A CAKE

When making a tiered cake, you need to make sure each cake is supported to prevent them from sinking and collapsing into the tier below. This is done using dowels which are pushed right down into the cake until they touch the board beneath. Choose the number of dowels you need per tier based on the size of the cake being added on top.

1   Use royal icing to fix the bottom tier of the cake on top of the covered cake drum.

2   Insert the number of cake dowels indicated in the table into the top of the cake, spacing them evenly and ensuring that, when the next tier is placed on top, they will all be covered.

3   Use a food colour pen to make a small mark on the side of each dowel at the point where it meets the top of the sugarpaste.

4   Remove the dowels, line them up and cut all of them to the height of the tallest mark. I find it easiest to cut a plastic dowel by gripping the mark between the blades of my kitchen scissors and twisting the dowel to create a shallow groove. You should then be able to snap it easily. Once trimmed, reinsert the dowels into the original holes.

5   Spread a little royal icing over the dowelled area and place the next tier on top, pressing it down gently to fix it in place.

6   Repeat steps 2–5 until all the tiers are fixed in place then set the cake aside to allow it to settle overnight.

SIZE OF TIER ABOVE	NUMBER OF DOWELS
10–15cm (4–6")	3
18–20.5cm (7–8")	4
23–25.5cm (9–10")	5

FLAT-ICING A CUPCAKE

Cupcakes often rise to different heights in their cases. Spreading a flat coating of buttercream over the top creates a neat and uniform surface on which to place cupcake toppers. It also helps to keep the cakes moist. Once you get the hang of it, you'll be able to do this job quickly and easily.

1 Hold the cupcake in your hand. Load the bottom edge of a cranked palette knife with buttercream and hold it against the centre of the top of the cupcake. Pull the spatula towards the edge of the cupcake case and towards yourself. The spatula should make contact with the top of the cupcake case. Scrape the excess buttercream from the base of the spatula into the mixing bowl.

2 Repeat step 1, working around the cupcake to completely cover the top with a smooth and level layer of buttercream.

ASSEMBLING A CAKE

I tend to start placing models on the cake as soon as I've finished working on them but I don't glue them down until I know their exact positions. I've been caught out a few times when I've glued a model in place and then realised that it's thrown off the composition or that I've not left enough room for another element going on the cake. It's frustrating to have to chip the model away, ruining the model and the cake surface, just to shift something over a little.

Once you have made the key models and are happy with their positions, use edible glue to fix them in place, or use royal icing if the models are already set and dry. After that, you can add all the little details to fill in the gaps, such as flowers, grass and other decorations.

MENDING A MODEL

There is nothing worse than creating a model and then something falling off! If the model is still soft you can use edible glue to bond the pieces together but once the model has dried out, the edible glue will no longer work. Fear not! You can still fix the model.

1 Use a small palette knife to combine a small amount of a matching coloured modelling paste with a little water to form a sticky putty.

2 Neatly spread the putty onto the edge that needs to be attached. Take care not to add too much putty as it will ooze out once pressed against the model.

3 Press the piece into place. Use a slightly damp paintbrush to remove any excess putty and neaten the edges.

TOP TIP

You can also use the putty to blend seams in your model. Once your model is dry, add the putty to the seam and use a Dresden tool to spread it into position.

STORING A MODEL

Time constraints can be a huge issue when it comes to decorating cakes and I'm often asked how long models can be kept for. As long as they're stored correctly, they can last for many months so there's really no need to have a last minute panic over creating a sugar figurine.

To make sure they stay looking their best, keep sugar models away from sunlight, moisture and dust. A simple cardboard cake box is perfect for storing your work until you're ready to use it, or even if you want to keep it as a keepsake.

TRANSPORTING A CAKE

I always try to have a cake finished at least 24 hours before delivery, that way I know it has had a chance to settle, all of the models are set, the glue bonding them to the cake has dried and nothing will shift. Most of the designs in this book require the cake to be assembled before it's decorated so make sure the cake is stacked and set before the 24 hour window.

I prefer to transport my cakes in heavy duty cake boxes. They're made from thicker cardboard and provide more protection than traditional white boxes. When assembling the box, leave one flap open so you can slide the cake in. The boxed cake should be placed on top of a non-slip mat on a flat surface in the empty boot of your car. I then pad the cake into position using fabric or cushions to wedge the cake box into the corner of the boot, that way it has less chance of skidding and toppling should the worst happen.

When driving, take corners slowly and try not to change speed too abruptly. You'll want to keep extra stopping distance between you and the car in front to avoid any harsh braking.

Until you're used to delivering cakes you will always be full of nerves but as long as you take it easy and follow these tips, you shouldn't have a problem. I've never had a cake collapse or a model break on me yet, touch wood!

TOP TIP

If the cake has any particularly fragile elements, for instance the flying ribbon on the 'Santa's Little Helpers' cake, place some food-safe foam underneath anything delicate to provide extra support for the journey.

TOP TIP

For particularly tall and wobbly models, try creating a sling from cling film.

You'll need a heavy-duty cake box with sides as high as the model. Cut a length of cling film that will reach from the edge of the box, around the model, and back to the edge, plus an extra 15cm (6"). Roll the cling film into a loose sausage and staple one end to the side of the box. Wrap the rest around the model and back towards the same edge, then staple the end in place. Repeat on the opposite side of the box. The model is now supported so, even if it does wobble on the journey, it'll only be able to move so much.

PROJECTS

CUTE COUPLE

This brew-tiful cake is perfect for tea lovers. The illustrative-style figures are simple to make and can be customised with different hair colour, skin colour and clothing.

MAN

SK HD Sugar Modelling Paste: 35g (1¼oz) Beige, 25g (>¾oz) Blue, 15g (½oz) Black, 5g (<¼oz) Brown and 25g (>¾oz) Turquoise

SK Edible Paints by Natasha Collins: Cherry Blossom, Conker and Jasmine

Paintbrush: no. 00

SK Designer Dust Food Colour: Pastel Pink

SK Sugar Florist Paste (SFP): 5g (<¼oz) White

WOMAN

SK HD Sugar Modelling Paste: 35g (1¼oz) Beige, 20g (¾oz) Orange, 25g (>¾oz) Pink and 25g (>¾oz) Red

SK Edible Paints by Natasha Collins: Cherry Blossom, Conker and Jasmine

Paintbrush: no. 00

SK Designer Dust Food Colour: Pastel Pink

SK Sugar Florist Paste (SFP): 5g (<¼oz) White

TEACUP CAKE

Drill fitted with a 5mm (¼") drill bit

Round cake drum: 30.5cm (12")

SK Sugarpaste: 400g (14oz) Ballerina Pink and 300g (10½oz) Bridal White

Airbrush kit

SK Professional Airbrush Colour: Pop Pink

Half-sphere sponge cake, 9cm (3½") deep: 15cm (6")

350g (12¼oz) buttercream

SK HD Sugar Modelling Paste: 45g (1½oz) Brown, 50g (1¾oz) Red and 220g (7¾oz) White

SK Professional Liquid Food Colour: Teddy Bear Brown

SK Professional Paste Food Colour: Teddy Bear Brown

SK Sugar Florist Paste (SFP): 20g (¾oz) White

SK Edible Paints by Natasha Collins: Cherry

PME Heart Cutters: 2cm, 2.5cm and 4cm (¾", 1" and 1½")

Round cutters: 5mm and 5cm (¼" and 2")

SK Professional Dust Food Colour: Chestnut

Round, fluted pastry cutter: 5.8cm (2¼")

1.5cm (½") width satin ribbon: 1m (1yd 3³/₈") red with white polka dots

3.5cm (1³/₈") tall. Use edible glue to fix the body in place (D).

4   Shaped a pea-sized ball of beige modelling paste into a cylinder and attach it to the top of the body to form the neck. Roll a small piece of turquoise modelling paste into a thin sausage and wrap this around the base of the cylinder to conceal the join.

5   To make the mini teacup, roll a pea-sized ball of White SFP and push a ball tool into the centre to form a well. Leaving the tool in the paste, use your fingers to work the paste up around the ball (E). Remove the ball tool and level the top of the cup. Push a small ball of brown modelling paste into the well and flatten it with your fingers. Glue the cup to the top of the man's leg.

6   Roll 3g (¹/₈oz) of beige modelling paste into a 5.5cm (2¼") long sausage shape, tapering one end slightly. Lightly pinch the narrower end of the sausage to form a spoon shape (F). Use a craft knife to cut out a thumb from one side of the hand (G). Use your fingers to smooth the cut edge. Thin the paste just below the hand to form the wrist. Bend the arm at the elbow.

7   Roll out the remaining turquoise modelling paste into a thin sheet and cut out a 2cm (¾") wide strip. Brush the top of the arm with edible glue then wrap the strip around it, ensuring the seam will be hidden underneath the arm (H). Trim away any excess. Use your fingers to work the top of the strip down and around the top of the arm to create a neat finish.

8   Glue the arm to the left side of the body, with the hand around the teacup. Roll a very fine sausage

of White SFP and wrap it around the hand to form the handle of the cup.

9   Repeat steps 6–7 to make a second arm, bending this one at the wrist rather than the elbow. Fix the arm to the right side of the body, with the hand on top of the cake (I).

10   Roll 25g (>¾oz) of beige modelling paste into a ball. Use the side of your finger to lightly indent a groove halfway up the ball (J). Use your fingers to smooth out the groove and remove any harsh lines.

11   Roll a small ball of beige modelling paste into a capsule shape and glue it in the centre of the face, positioning it horizontally along the lower edge of the groove.

12   Lightly push a small ball tool into the left side of the face, just above the nose, and move it up and down to create an oval-shaped indentation. Repeat to create a second indentation on the right side of the face (K).

13   Push a ball tool into either side of the head to create holes for the ears. Roll a small ball of beige modelling paste into a teardrop and glue the pointed end into one of the holes. Use a small ball tool to push the ear into the head, creating the cupped shape. Repeat to add a second ear on the other side of the head.

14   Use Conker edible paint and a no. 00 paintbrush to add the eyes and eyebrows, leaving a small circle in the top right corner of each eye unpainted (L). Use Cherry Blossom edible paint to add a curved mouth. Dip a small ball tool in Jasmine edible paint and fill in the unpainted

MAN

1   Roll 25g (>¾oz) of blue modelling paste into a slightly tapered 6cm (2³/₈") long sausage for the trousers. Flatten the ends of the shape. Run a Dresden tool along the centre of the shape, stopping 1cm (³/₈") short of the top, to create two legs (A). Gently bend the trousers at the knee and use edible glue to fix them over the edge of your chosen cake (B). Push a cocktail stick through the top of the trousers and into the cake to provide support.

2   Divide a marble-sized ball of black modelling paste in half. Roll each piece into a teardrop then flatten them slightly to form shoe shapes. Use edible glue to fix the two shoes together then glue them to the bottom of the trousers. Support the feet as they dry.

3   Roll 20g (¾oz) of turquoise modelling paste into an egg shape. Flatten the base of the egg then use your fingers to stretch and thin the edge so that it fits around the trousers (C). The finished shape should be

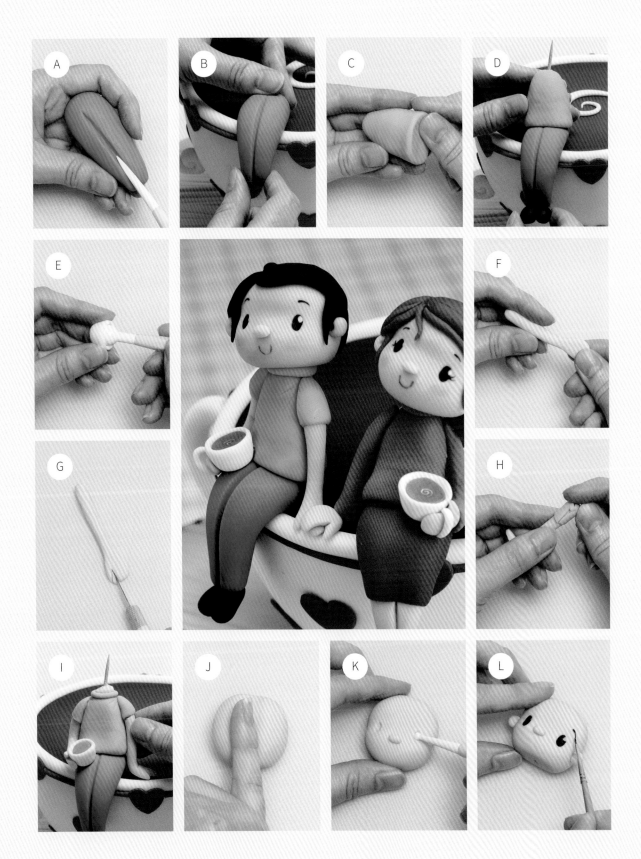

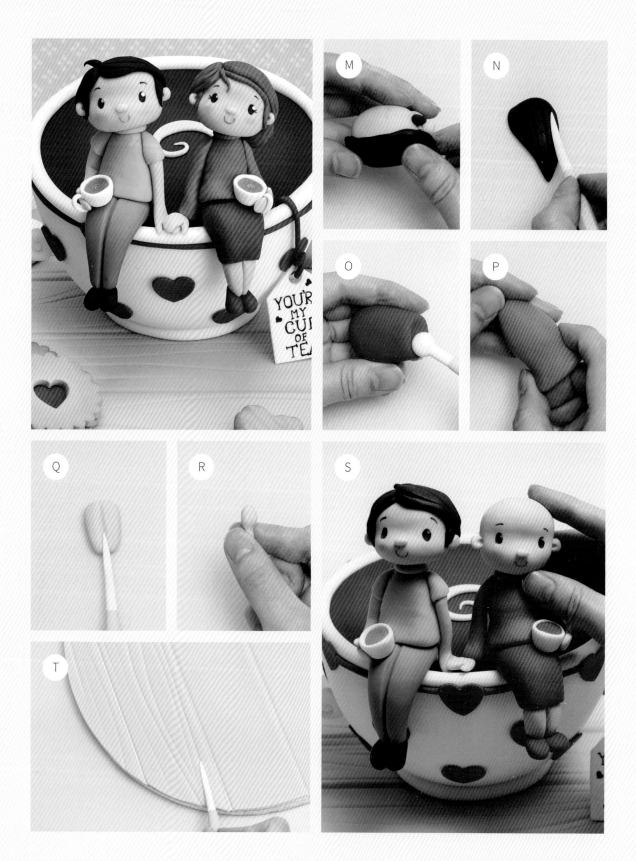

circles. Brush the cheeks with Pastel Pink dust food colour.

15 Flatten a marble-sized ball of black modelling paste into a disc and use edible glue to fix it to the back of the head (M). Use the pointed end of a Dresden tool to draw lines in the surface of the paste, giving the impression of hair. Roll two small pieces of black modelling paste into teardrops and glue one in front of each ear.

16 Use edible glue to fix the head to the neck, tilting it slightly.

17 Roll a marble-sized ball of black modelling paste into a teardrop and flatten it. Use a Dresden tool to draw lines in the surface of the paste (N). Glue the hair on the right side of the head. Repeat to make a smaller teardrop and attach it to the left side of the head. Finish with a small teardrop sticking up from the crown.

WOMAN

1 Roll 20g (¾oz) of red modelling paste into a tapered cylinder 4.5cm (1¾") long. Push a ball tool into the narrower end of the shape to open it out (O). Bend the skirt at the knee and fix it in place on the top edge of your chosen cake using edible glue.

2 Repeat step 3 from the Man instructions to make the body, using 20g (¾oz) of pink modelling paste. Use your fingers to thin the waist slightly (P). Glue the body on top of the skirt and push a cocktail stick through the figure and into the cake for support.

3 Shape 4g (<¼oz) of beige modelling paste into a tapered cylinder 2cm (¾") long. Run a Dresden tool down the centre of the shape to create two legs (Q). Glue the legs into the narrow end of the skirt, supporting them until secure. Repeat step 2 from the Man instructions to add a pair of shoes using a marble-sized ball of red modelling paste.

4 Repeat step 5 from the Man instructions to make and attach a mini teacup.

5 Divide 5g (<¼oz) of pink modelling paste in half and roll each piece into a 4cm (1½") long cone. Push a ball tool into the wider end of each shape. Bend one arm at the elbow and set them aside until needed.

6 Roll a pea-sized piece of beige modelling paste into a ball and pinch out a wrist shape (R). Flatten the remaining ball and cut out the thumb. Use your fingers to smooth the cut edges. Trim the wrist and glue it into the well in one of the arms. Repeat to add a hand to the second arm.

7 Glue the arms to the shoulders so the left hand is on top of the man's hand and the right hand is around the mini teacup. Roll a very fine sausage of White SFP and wrap it around the hand to form the handle of the cup.

8 Repeat steps 10–14 from the Man instructions to make the woman's head. Add two eyelashes to the edge of each eye using Conker edible paint. Use edible glue to fix the head to the neck, tilting it slightly (S).

9 Repeat steps 15 and 17 from Man instructions using orange modelling paste. Roll a piece of orange modelling paste into a long, tapered sausage. Glue the paste along the front of the hair, starting at the parting and following the hairline down to the ears. Add one small teardrop shape running from the parting onto the forehead.

10 For the bun, roll a marble-sized ball of orange modelling paste into an ovoid. Use a Dresden tool to draw lines over the surface of the paste and attach it to the back of the head.

COVERING

1 Use a 5mm (¼") drill bit to bore a hole in the cake drum 12cm (4¾") from the edge. Use a cake dowel to widen the hole.

2 Cover the cake drum using 400g (14oz) of Ballerina Pink sugarpaste, (see page 30).

3 Use the pointed end of a Dresden tool to draw six evenly spaced horizontal lines across the surface of the sugarpaste. Using light pressure, create a woodgrain effect by drawing short, curved lines along each section (T).

4 Half-fill the airbrush cup with Pop Pink airbrush food colour. Hold the tip of the airbrush 15cm (6") away from the covered drum and gently pull back the trigger to release the spray of colour. Build up the colour around the edges of the drum and the edges of each plank.

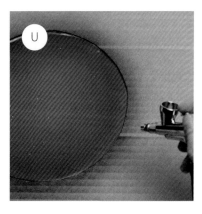

5   Cut a cake dowel to a 7.5cm (3")
    length and insert it into the hole in
the drum. Set the covered drum aside
to firm for 24 hours.

6   Turn the 15cm (6") half-sphere
    cake upside down and trim away
the top of the dome to create a flat
surface. Use the buttercream to fill the
cake and apply a thin crumb coat to
all sides. Refrigerate the cake for four
hours before covering.

7   Cover the cake using 300g
    (10½oz) of Bridal White
sugarpaste (see page 28). Set the cake
aside to firm for 24 hours.

8   Once firm, carefully flip the cake
    over so the widest flat side is
uppermost and place it over the dowel
in the drum. Fix the cake to the drum
using a small amount of royal icing.

9   Apply a thin layer of buttercream
    to the top of the cake. Knead
together 45g (1½oz) of Brown
modelling paste and 15g (½oz) of
White modelling paste. Roll out the
paste to a 2mm (1/16") thickness and cut
out a 15cm (6") disc. Place the disc on
top of the cake and smooth it into place
with a cake smoother.

10 Cut out a neat 15cm (6") circle
    from the middle of a thick sheet
of cardboard. Fill the airbrush cup with
Teddy Bear Brown liquid food colour.
Lay the card over the top of the cake
so that only the area inside the cup
is visible. Hold the tip of the airbrush
15cm (6") away from the surface of the
sugarpaste and build up the colour
around the edges of the stencil (U).

DECORATION

1   Knead a small amount of Teddy
    Bear Brown paste food colour
into 5g (<¼oz) of white modelling
paste. Roll the pale brown paste into
a tapered sausage then curl it into a
spiral. Glue the spiral in the centre of
the mug.

2   Roll 20g (¾oz) of white modelling
    paste into a 1cm (3/8") diameter
sausage. Glue the sausage around the
base of the cake.

3   Roll 50g (1¾oz) of white
    modelling paste into a sausage
52cm (20½") long. Hold a cake
smoother against either side of the
sausage and gently compress it to
flatten the sides. Continue along the

length of the sausage, then turn it on
its side and repeat to create a square
prism. Glue the strip around the top
edge of the cup, ensuring the join is at
the front, to the right of the centre.

4   Roll 5g (<¼oz) of red modelling
    paste into a fine sausage 52cm
(20½") long. Glue the paste around the
join between the cup and the rim. Roll
out 20g (¾oz) of red modelling paste
into a thin sheet and cut out 18 hearts
using the 2.5cm (1") cutter. Glue the
hearts over the surface of the cup.

5   For the handle, roll 10g (¼oz) of
    White SFP into a sausage 9cm
(3½") long. Taper one end slightly and
curl it up to create a spiral. Slightly
flatten the other end of the sausage
and bend it into a C shape. Use edible
glue to fix the handle on the left side
of the cake (V). Insert a cocktail stick
through the curled end of the handle
and into the cake to hold it in place.
Use food-grade foam to support the
handle as it dries.

6   To make the teabag tag, roll out
    10g (¼oz) of White SFP into a
thin sheet. Cut out a 5cm x 3.5cm (2"
x 1 3/8") rectangle and cut one end to
a point. Cut a hole in the pointed end

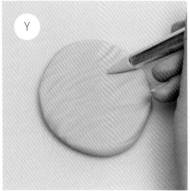

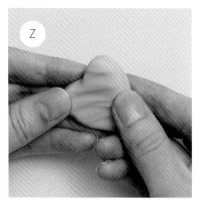

using a 5mm (¼") round cutter. Use a no. 00 paintbrush and Cherry edible paint to write 'YOU'RE MY CUP OF TEA' on the tag, then add some small hearts (W). Set the tag aside to dry for three hours.

BISCUITS

1   Knead a little Teddy Bear Brown paste food colour into 100g (3½oz) of white modelling paste. Roll out the paste to a 4mm (³/₁₆") thickness and cut out four scalloped discs using the 5.8cm (2¼") fluted cutter. Use the 2cm (¾") heart cutter to cut out a heart from the centre of two of the discs (X).

2   Roll out the remaining paste to an 8mm (³/₈") thickness and use a silicone-tipped modelling tool to create a rippled pattern in the surface (Y). Cut out two hearts using the 4cm (1½") heart cutter. Use your fingers to smooth and round off the top edge (Z).

3   Brush the edges of the biscuits with Chestnut dust food colour.

4   Roll out 20g (¾oz) of red modelling paste into a thin sheet and cut out two 5cm (2") discs. Use edible glue to fix one red disc to each scalloped disc, then glue the scalloped discs with the hearts cut out on top. Set the biscuits aside to firm.

SUGAR CUBES

1   Roll 10g (¼oz) of white modelling paste into a ball. Press the paste between two cake smoothers to flatten the sides then turn the ball and repeat to create a cube.

2   Use a small ball tool to mark dimples in the surface of the cube. Repeat to make three white cubes.

FINISHING TOUCHES

1   Build the figures over the edge of the teacup.

2   Glue the first sugar cube to the cake drum, positioning it underneath the seam on the rim of the cup. Glue the teabag tag to the front of the sugar cube.

3   Roll 10g (¼oz) of red modelling paste into a 3mm (¹/₈") diameter sausage shape. Glue one end of the sausage over the seam on the rim of the cup and feed the other end through the hole in the tag. Loop the loose end up and wrap it around itself several times to secure.

4   Glue the biscuits and remaining sugar cubes in place on the drum.

5   Wrap red ribbon around the edge of the cake drum and fix it in place with double-sided tape.

TOP TIP

Add a little Poppy gel colour to some SK Piping Gel to create an effective jammy filling for your biscuits.

CLASSMATES

This tutorial shows how to make both adults and children in various seated positions. The book cakes are a great staple too and can be adapted to whatever subject matter you prefer.

TEACHER

SK HD Sugar Modelling Paste: 55g (2oz) Beige, 5g (<¼oz) Black, 5g (<¼oz) Brown, 40g (1½oz) Orange, 15g (½oz) Pink, 75g (2½oz) Red, 100g (3½oz) White

Food colour pen: black

FMM Carnation Cutter: 3.8cm (1½")

SK Quality Food Colour (QFC) Dust: Pink

BOY

SK Sugar Dough: 30g (1oz) Blue

SK HD Sugar Modelling Paste: 50g (1¾oz) Beige, 25g (>¾oz) Black, 5g (<¼oz) Brown and 35g (1¼oz) White

PME Star Cutter: 2cm (¾")

SK Quality Food Colour (QFC) Dust: Pink

Round cutter: 5cm (2")

GIRL

SK HD Sugar Modelling Paste: 2g (<⅛oz) Beige, 30g (1oz) Black, 40g (1½oz) Brown, 35g (1oz) Pink, 5g (<¼oz) Turquoise, 10g (¼oz) White and 25g (>¾oz) Yellow

Square cutter: 3.5cm (1³/₈")

Food colour pen: black

Assorted dust food colours

BOOK CAKES

Round cake drum: 25.5cm (14")

SK Sugarpaste: 400g (14oz) Mocha Cream, 140g (5oz) Spa Blue, 770g (1lb 11oz) White and 400g (14oz) Zesty Orange

Stainless steel icing ruler: 40.5cm (16")

SK Professional Dust Food Colour: Chestnut

1.5cm (½") width grosgrain ribbon: 1m (1yd 3³/₈") brown

Rectangular cake boards: 2 x 20.5cm x 15cm (8" x 6")

2 rectangular, filled sponge cakes, 7.5cm (3") deep: 20.5cm x 15cm (8" x 6")

450g (1lb) buttercream

Spare rectangular cake drum

Marzipan spacer

SK Sugar Florist Paste (SFP): 30g (1oz) White

Alphabet cutters: uppercase

SK HD Sugar Modelling Paste: 5g (<¼oz) Beige, 15g (½oz) Green, 40g (1½oz) White and 15g (½oz) Yellow

Square cutter: 3.5cm (1³/₈")

Food colour pen: black

SK Professional Dust Food Colours: Sunflower

Assorted dust food colours

TEACHER

1 Roll 70g (2½oz) of red modelling paste into a 21cm (8¼") long sausage with a thicker centre and slightly tapered ends. Bend the paste in half and gently bend each leg at the knee (A). Push a ball tool approximately 5mm (¼") into the end of each leg and use a Dresden tool to mark creases at the knees. Glue the legs on top of your chosen cake (B).

2 For the shoes, divide a 5g (<¼oz) ball of red modelling paste in half. Roll the balls into capsule shapes and gently flatten them. Press a ball tool into the top of each shoe to form a well (C).

3 For the ankles, divide a 5g (<¼oz) ball of beige modelling paste in half and roll it into a sausage with a narrow centre. Bend the shape in half and shape one end to fit the well in the shoe (D). Glue the paste into the shoe then shape the ankle to fit inside the hollow in the trouser leg, securing it with edible glue (E). Repeat to make and attach the second foot.

4 For the body, shape 60g (2oz) of white modelling paste into a 6cm (2³⁄₈") tall cone then flatten the base and the tip. Use your fingers to pinch and thin the bottom edge so that it fits over the top of the legs (F). Glue the body in place. Push a wooden barbecue skewer down through the body and into the cake leaving approximately 2.5cm (1") protruding from the top.

5 To make the teacher's book, shape 12g (½oz) of white modelling paste into a 3.5cm x 5cm (1³⁄₈" x 2") rectangle. Use a Dresden tool to draw a crease across the centre of the book. Soften the crease and the edges of the pages using your fingers. Use a Dresden tool to score lines in the sides of the book. Roll out 15g (½oz) of pink modelling paste to a 1mm (<¹⁄₁₆") thickness. Attach the centre of the book to the rolled-out paste and trim it to fit. Lightly bend the book in the centre then add two lines on either side of the spine. Use a black food colour pen to draw lines of text inside the book. Push a cocktail stick into the leg then feed the book over the top and use edible glue to secure it in place.

6 For the hands, divide 4g (<¼oz) of beige modelling paste into two balls. Gently pinch and roll the paste between your fingers to extrude a point from one side (G). Lightly flatten the rounded area and shape it into an oval. Use a craft knife to cut away a small triangle from each hand to create the thumb (H). Roll the thumb between your fingers to round off the edges. Lightly stretch the piece of paste where the fingers will be and cut into it three times to create the fingers. Round off the cut edges (I). Roll the wrist between your fingers to thin and shape it. Trim the area beyond the wrist so that it will fit neatly inside the sleeve. Repeat to make a second hand.

7 Roll 10g (¼oz) of white modelling paste into a 7.5cm (3") long sausage, tapered at one end. Push a 6mm (¼") diameter ball tool into the widest end of the sausage to open up the sleeve (J). Bend the sausage into a right angle halfway along its length. Repeat to create the second arm. Fix the wrists inside the sleeves using edible glue.

8 Glue the arms to the shoulders, with the right hand supporting the book and the left hand resting on top of the page. Use a Dresden tool to mark creases at the elbows.

9 Roll out a small piece of white modelling paste into a thin sheet and cut out a flower shape using the Carnation cutter. Glue the flower shape over the top of the body and arms (K).

10 Roll a pea-sized ball of beige modelling paste into a cylinder and glue it on top of the flower to make the neck. Wrap a thin sausage of white modelling paste around the base of the neck to conceal the join.

11 Roll 40g (1½oz) of beige modelling paste into an egg shape. Use the side of your hand to lightly indent a groove halfway up the egg (L). Use your fingers to smooth out the groove and remove any harsh edges. Place your index fingers into the groove on the face, leaving a small gap between them for the bridge of the nose, and lightly press down (M). Smooth away the edges of the indentations. Push the broad end of a Dresden tool into the face and gently rock it from side to side and upwards to open up the eye sockets (N).

12 Roll a small piece of beige modelling paste into a capsule shape and glue it to the centre of the face for the nose.

13 Push a small ball tool into each side of the head to make indentations for the ears. Roll two small pieces of beige modelling paste into teardrops and glue them into the ear holes. Push a ball tool into the centre of each ear to open them out (O).

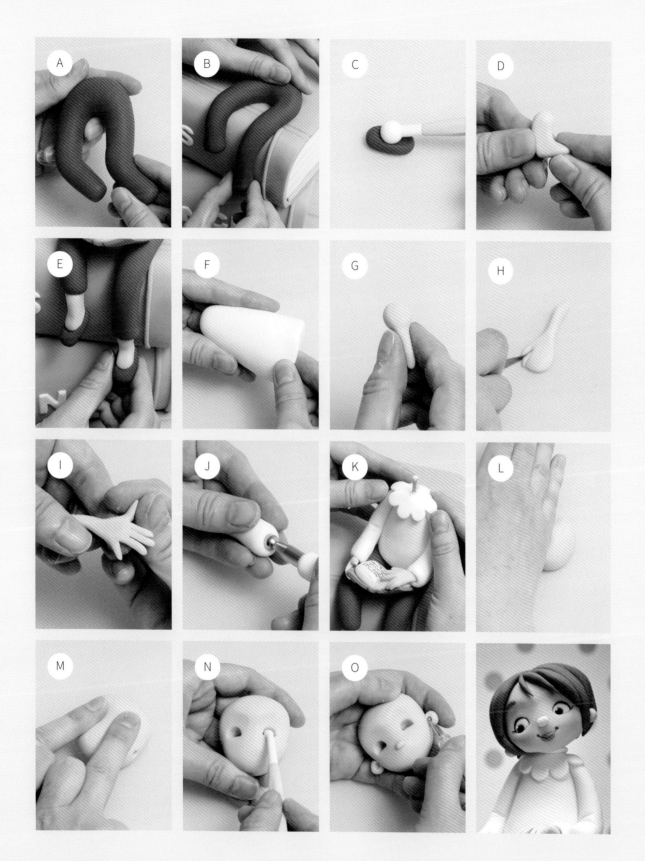

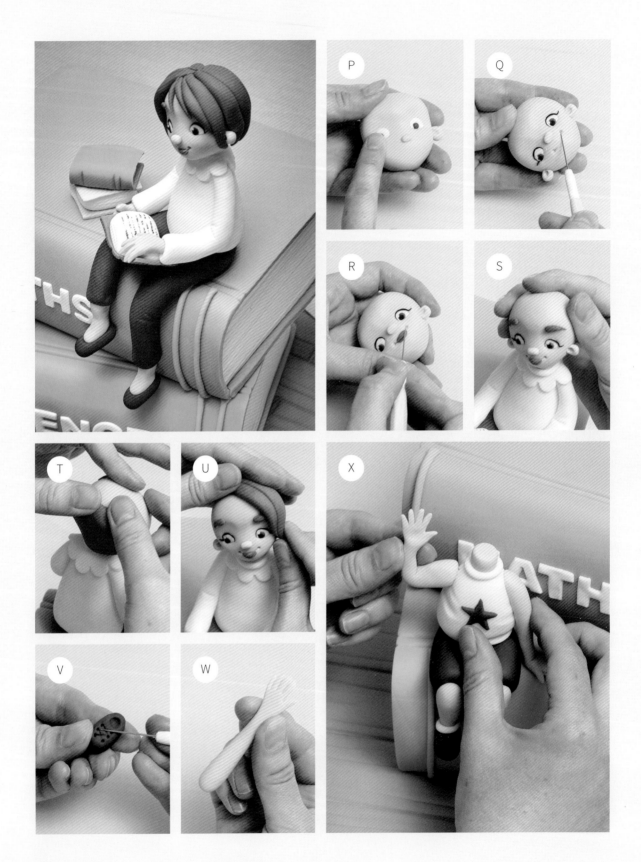

14 Fill each eye socket with a small piece of white modelling paste. Push a ball tool into the bottom left corner of each eye to form a well. Fill the well with a small ball of brown modelling paste (P). Use a smaller ball tool to create a small well in the centre of the brown circle and fill it with a small ball of black modelling paste. Add two very small dots of white modelling paste to each eye. Roll two very fine tapered sausages of black modelling paste and glue them around the upper eyelids to form the eyelashes.

15 Press a small ball tool into the lower half of the face on either side of the nose. Place the tip of a scribing tool into each indent and press down lightly to draw the ends of a smile (Q). Roll a small piece of pink modelling paste into an oval then use the scribing tool to continue the smile line over the paste and create two lips (R).

16 Roll two small, tapered sausages of orange modelling paste and glue them above the eyes for the eyebrows.

17 Lightly brush the cheeks with Pink dust food colour. Push the head onto the skewer and check the height of the neck, trimming away any excess, if necessary. Fix the head in position using edible glue (S).

18 If the back of the model's head has flattened, shape 8g (¼oz) of orange modelling paste into a shallow dome and glue it to on top (T).

19 For the fringe roll one 5g (<¼oz) and one 3g (<⅛oz) piece of orange modelling paste into

tapered sausages, glue them together then fix them in over the forehead (U). Repeat for the other side.

20 Divide 20g (¾oz) of orange modelling paste into eight even balls. Roll the balls into tapered sausages and glue them over the back of the head. Glue two small teardrops at the parting.

BOY

1 Roll 25g (>¾oz) of Blue Sugar Dough into a 9cm (3½") long sausage and bend it in half. Push a ball tool into each end to create a shallow well.

2 For the lower legs, divide 6g (¼oz) of beige modelling paste in half and roll each piece into a 3.5cm (1⅜") long tapered sausage.

3 Shape two small pieces of Blue Sugar Dough into capsules. Press a ball tool into one end of each piece to form a well. Make two rows of three indentations on each shoe then join them using a scribing tool to represent laces (V). Glue one shoe to the narrow end of each leg. Glue a thin sausage of white modelling paste around the top of each shoe to conceal the join. Fix the knees into the wells in the shorts. Glue the completed legs on top of the cake.

4 For the body, roll 30g (1oz) of white modelling paste into an egg shape. Flatten the base of the egg and glue it on top of the legs. Push a wooden barbecue skewer down through the body and into the cake. Use a Dresden tool to mark creases in the T-shirt. Roll out a small amount of Blue Sugar Dough thinly and cut out a

star using the 2cm (¾") cutter. Glue the star to the front of the the T-shirt.

5 Roll a pea-sized ball of beige modelling paste into a cylinder and glue it at the top of the body. Fix a very fine sausage of white modelling paste around the base of the neck to conceal the join.

6 To make the arms, divide an 8g (¼oz) ball of beige modelling paste in half and roll each piece into a capsule shape. Place your hand over the paste so that final 1cm (⅜") of the capsule is not covered, and continue to roll the rest of the paste until it is 6cm (2⅜") long in its entirety. Flatten the wider end of each arm and follow step 6 from the Teacher instructions to make the hands (W).

7 Glue the left arm to the side of the body, with the hand resting on the top of the cake. Bend the right arm at the elbow. Use a Dresden tool to mark the palm of the hand. Set the right arm aside to firm for 30 minutes. Once the arm is firm, push a 3.5cm (1⅜") length of cocktail stick into the shoulder. Brush a little edible glue around the stick then feed the arm over it and glue it in place (X).

8 Shape two small balls of white modelling paste into rugby balls. Flatten the balls between your fingers and glue them in place over the tops of the arms to make the sleeves.

9 To make the head, follow steps 11–14 from the Teacher instructions using 30g (1oz) of beige modelling paste, this time adding the irises and pupils to the top right edge of each eye.

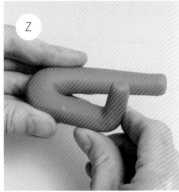

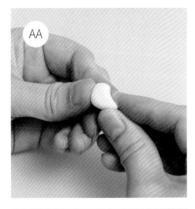

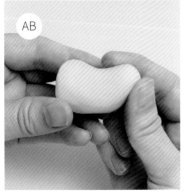

10 Use a Dresden tool to draw the mouth. Add a small indentation at each end using a mini ball tool.

11 Roll two small, tapered sausages of black modelling paste and glue them above the eyes for the eyebrows.

12 Shape 10g (¼oz) of black modelling paste to fit over the back of the head, up to the ears, then glue it in place. Glue a small teardrop of black modelling paste in front of each ear. Roll out 10g (¼oz) of black modelling paste into a thin sheet and cut out a 5cm (2") disc. Gently stretch the disc into an oval that will cover the top of the boy's head. Use a sharp knife to cut small V-shaped nicks from the edges of the disc. Draw lines radiating from the centre with a Dresden tool (Y). Glue the shape on top of the boy's head. Finish with a small teardrop of black modelling paste at the crown.

GIRL

1 Roll 30g (1oz) of pink modelling paste into a 16cm (6¼") sausage with a thicker centre and slightly tapered ends. Bend the paste in half. Bend one leg into a right angle halfway along its length (Z). Use a Dresden tool to mark creases at the knees and along the side of each leg.

2 For the shoes, shape two small balls of white modelling paste into capsules and bend them slightly in the middle (AA). Use a Dresden tool to draw a line around the bottom edge of each shoe for the sole. Glue one shoe to the end of each leg.

3 For the body, roll 25g (>¾oz) of yellow modelling paste into an egg. Use your fingers to pinch and thin the bottom edge of the shape so that it fits over the legs. Bend the chest upwards (AB). Glue the body to the top of the legs and insert a cocktail stick through the neck and down into the body. Add creases at the waist using a Dresden tool.

4 Roll a pea-sized ball of brown modelling paste into a cylinder and glue it to the top of the body. Fix a very fine sausage of yellow modelling paste around the base of the neck to conceal the join.

5 Roll out a small piece of white modelling paste into a thin sheet and cut out a square using the 3.5cm (1³⁄₈") square cutter. Set the square aside to firm for one hour. Mix dust food colours with a little clear alcohol, e.g. vodka or gin, and use them to paint 'Thank You Teacher' on the white square (see page 53).

6 Roll a small sausage of turquoise modelling paste and trim it to a 1.5cm (½") length. Roll a small cone of beige modelling paste and glue it to the end of the sausage. Glue a tiny piece of the turquoise modelling paste to the tip of the cone.

7 Follow step 6 from the Boy instructions to make the girl's arms using 8g (¼oz) of brown modelling paste. Bend each arm at the elbow. Glue the turquoise pencil to the palm of the right hand. Glue the fingers around the pencil. Place the 'Thank You Teacher' drawing in front of the girl. Glue the arms to the shoulders, positioning the left hand above the drawing and the right hand resting on its surface. Allow the model to firm overnight.

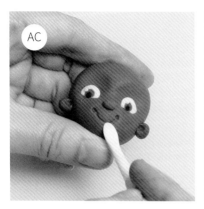

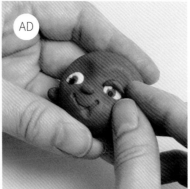

8   To make the head, follow steps 11–14 from the Teacher instructions using 25g (>¾oz) of brown modelling paste.

9   Use a Dresden tool to draw in the mouth. Add a small indentation at each end using a mini ball tool. Press the wide end of a Dresden tool into the bottom of the smile, slightly to the left (AC).

10   Roll two tapered sausages of brown modelling paste and flatten them to form semi-circles. Glue one semi-circle along the top of each eye to form the eyelids (AD). Glue a fine, tapered sausage of black modelling paste along the base of each eyelid.

11   Roll two small, tapered sausages of black modelling paste and glue them above the eyes for the eyebrows.

12   Roll a small piece of pink modelling paste into a teardrop and glue it into the well below the mouth. Draw a line down the centre of the tongue using a Dresden tool.

13   For the hair, shape 10g (¼oz) of black modelling paste to fit the back of the head. Cut a 2cm (¾") long notch into one side of the shape to make the parting (AE). Glue the paste to the back of the head with the parting positioned centrally on top, leaving a little brown modelling paste visible (AF). Draw in hair lines with a Dresden tool.

14   Roll two small pieces of black modelling paste into balls and use a ball tool to add texture to the surface. Flatten two smaller balls of pink modelling paste into discs and glue them on either side of the parting. Cut a cocktail stick into two 2cm (¾") lengths and push one into the centre of each disc. Push the two textured balls over the cocktail sticks and glue them to the discs (AG).

15   To finish, roll thin sausages of black modelling paste and glue them along the hairline. Glue a small cone of black modelling paste in the centre of the hairline curling the tip over.

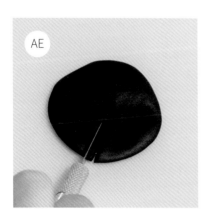

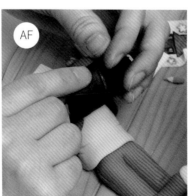

DRUM

1   Cover the drum using 400g (4oz) of Mocha Cream sugarpaste (see page 30).

2   Mark nine evenly spaced horizontal lines across the surface of the sugarpaste using the icing ruler. Using light pressure, draw in a woodgrain pattern between the lines with a Dresden tool (AH). Set the covered drum aside to firm for 24 hours.

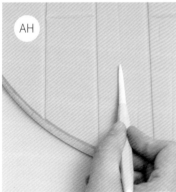

3   Once firm, brush the edges of each plank and the drum with Chestnut dust food colour.

4   Wrap brown grosgrain ribbon around the edge of the drum and fix it in place with double-sided tape.

BOOK CAKES

1   Spread a small amount of buttercream over the first 20.5cm x 15cm (8" x 6") cake board and place the first rectangular cake on top. Use a serrated knife to round off one of the longer sides. Carve the opposite side so it curves inwards. Spread a thin layer of buttercream over the cake and use a scraper to create a smooth surface and neat edges. Repeat to carve and crumb coat the second cake. Chill the cakes for approximately four hours.

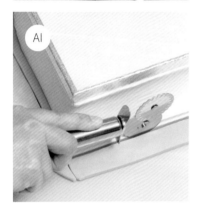

2   Brush a little cooled, boiled water over the two shorter sides and the inward-curving side of one of the cakes. Roll 250g (8¾oz) of Bridal White sugarpaste into a large sausage shape. Using a rolling pin, roll the sugarpaste out into a strip approximately 9cm x 51cm (3½" x 20"). Use a cutting wheel to cut a straight edge along one side. Gently lift the paste and attach it to the moistened sides of the cake. Smooth the surface of the sugarpaste and work it into the curve. Gently press the icing ruler along the length of all three sides to mimic the pages of a book. Repeat to cover the sides of the second cake.

3   Knead together 140g (5oz) of Spa Blue sugarpaste and 280g (9¾oz) of Bridal White sugarpaste to make a pale blue colour. Use a pastry brush to apply a little cooled, boiled water to the top and spine of the first cake. Roll out the pale blue sugarpaste to a 4mm (³/₁₆") thickness. Lay the sugarpaste over the cake and smooth it with your hands.

4   Place a sheet of baking parchment followed by a spare cake drum on top of the cake. In one swift movement, flip the cake over so that it sits upside down. Lay a spacer along one of the short edges of the cake and run the cutting wheel along the edge of the spacer, trimming away the excess sugarpaste and leaving a small overhang (AI). Repeat to trim away the excess sugarpaste on the other short side of the cake and the longer, inward-curving side. Brush a little cooled, boiled water over the rounded edge and wrap the edge of the sugarpaste sheet around it. Trim away the excess with a sharp knife. Flip the cake back over again and smooth the surface.

5　Repeat steps 2–4 to cover the second book cake with 400g (7oz) of Zesty Orange sugarpaste.

6　Roll the remaining pale blue sugarpaste into a long sausage then roll it out to a 4mm ($^3/_{16}$") thickness and 50.8cm (20") length. Brush a little edible glue around the bottom edge of the pages on the blue book. Use the cutting wheel to cut a straight edge along the length of the sugarpaste strip. Wrap the paste around the bottom edge of the cake and gently press with a smoother to adhere. Use the spacer and a cutting wheel to trim away the excess paste, leaving an overhang to match the top edge. Repeat with the orange cake. Leave the cakes to firm for 24 hours.

7　Roll a long, thin sausage of pale blue sugarpaste and cut it into three 9cm (3½") lengths. Glue one strip 1cm ($^3/_8$") from the left edge of the spine. Glue the second strip 1cm ($^3/_8$") from the right edge then add the final strip 1cm ($^3/_8$") in from the previous one. Repeat using the Zesty Orange sugarpaste on the orange cake.

8　For the writing, roll out 30g (1oz) of White SFP into a thin sheet. Use the cutters to cut out the words 'MATHS' and 'SCIENCE', or your chosen titles. Place a 15cm (6") rolling pin against the bottom of the spine and use it as a guide, attaching the letters to the books immediately above it.

9　Use royal icing to carefully secure the pale blue cake at an angle towards the back of the covered drum. Dowel the blue cake following the instructions on page 31. Spread royal icing over the dowelled area and place the orange cake on top, at an angle.

10　Build the teacher and boy on top of the orange and blue books. Attach the girl to the cake drum in front of the books.

ART MATERIALS

1　Roll out 20g (¾oz) of white modelling paste into a thin sheet and cut out two squares using the 3.5cm (1³⁄₈") square cutter. Set the squares aside to firm for one hour. Once firm, use a black food colour pen to draw a house on one square and a sun with a smiley face on the other. Mix Sunflower dust food colour with a little clear alcohol, e.g. vodka or gin, and use it to fill in the sun. Make more paints in the same way using various dust food colours and use them to colour in the house.

2　To make the colouring pencils, roll small sausages of various colours of modelling paste. Trim each sausage to a different length between 8mm and 1.8cm (¼" and ½"). Roll small cones of beige modelling paste and glue to the end of each sausage. Glue a tiny piece of the corresponding coloured paste to the tip of each cone. Glue the sun and house drawings to the drum, along with the pencils.

3　For the closed books, shape 10g (¼oz) of white modelling paste into a 2.5cm x 3.5cm (1" x 1³⁄₈") oblong. Draw page lines on three of the sides using a Dresden tool. Roll out 15g (½oz) of green modelling paste into a thin sheet and glue the white oblong on top. Trim the green paste so that it is just wider than the white oblong and long enough to wrap over the top. Brush edible glue over the spine and top of the book then flip over the green paste to cover it. Trim away any excess paste. Draw three grooves in the spine of the book. Repeat using 15g (½oz) of yellow modelling paste to cover a second book. Glue the books next to the teacher.

YOGA BUDDIES

These characters are perfect for the yogi in your life. Not only are they fun figures but they also teach you how to create simple armatures to give your models more lifelike poses.

YOU WILL NEED

COBRA POSE

Floral wires: 18-gauge white

Floral tape: white

SK Cocoform Modelling Chocolate: 75g (2½oz) White

SK Quality Food Colour (QFC) Dusts: Pink and Purple

SK HD Sugar Modelling Paste: 25g (>¾oz) Black, 40g (1½oz) Brown and 2g (<¼oz) White

LOTUS LADY

SK HD Sugar Modelling Paste: 35g (1¼oz) Beige, 5g (<¼oz) Black, 30g (1oz) Blue, 5g (<¼oz) Turquoise and 140g (5oz) White

DOG

SK HD Sugar Modelling Paste: 2g (<¼oz) Black, 2g (<¼oz) Pink and 40g (1½oz) White

SK Professional Food Colour: Teddy Bear Brown

Food colour pen: Black

PARK CAKE

SK Sugarpaste: 2.5kg (5lb 8¾oz) Iced Mint

CMC Cellulose Gum

Round, buttercream-covered cakes, 12.5cm (5") deep: 12.5cm and 18cm (5" and 7")

Round cake drum: 33cm (13")

SK HD Modelling Paste: 35g (1¼oz) Brown, 15g (½oz) Pink, 10g (¼oz) Turquoise, 70g (2½oz) White and 20g (¾oz) Yellow

SK Sugar Florist Paste (SFP): 25g (>¾oz) Black and 20g (¾oz) White

FMM Tappits: Script Upper and Lower Case

SK Designer Paste Food Colour: Sunny Lime

1.5cm (½") width satin ribbon: 1.05m (42") Iced Mint

COBRA POSE

1 Cut two 16cm (6¼") and two 18cm (7") lengths of 18-gauge white floral wire. Wrap a layer of white floral tape around each of the shorter wires, then use the tape to bind the two pieces of wire together. Bend the shorter wire to a 90° angle 6cm (2⅜") from the end. Wrap a layer of floral tape 6cm (2⅜") along the length of each of the longer wires. Bend the longer wires to a 90° angle 4cm (1½") from the end.

2 Place the shorter wire on your work surface with the 6cm (2⅜") length pointing upwards. Hold the 4cm (1½") section of one of the longer wires against the 6cm (2⅜") section of the shorter wire, lining up the end with the bend. Use floral tape to fix the wire in place. Repeat to attach the second longer wire to the opposite side (A).

3 Colour 40g (1½oz) of White Cocoform with Pink dust food colour. Roll the paste into a slightly tapered sausage 9cm (3½") in length. Use your little finger to mark a groove halfway along the shape (B). Use a Dresden tool to draw a line dividing the two legs (C). Shape the paste with your fingers to enhance the calves and bottom then smooth away the harsh lines left by the tool. Push the legs onto the 10cm (4") length of wire on the armature. Shape the Cocoform to fit the wire, leaving a 2mm (¹⁄₁₆") section visible at the end (D). Add creases around the knee area with a Dresden tool.

4 Roll two small sausages of brown modelling paste and shape them into feet. Use a sharp craft knife to mark in the toes. Glue the feet at the end of the trousers (E).

5 Colour 35g (1¼oz) of White Cocoform with Purple dust food colour. Roll 30g (1oz) of the purple Cocoform into an egg shape then use your fingers to stretch and thin the edge of the wider end so that it fits around the top of the trousers. Place the t-shirt on its front and cut a cross shape into it, using the armature for reference (F). Push the Cocoform onto the armature, with the cut side facing the feet (G). Use your fingers to blend the Cocoform around the armature smoothing away the cuts. Mark creases in the t-shirt using a Dresden tool. Bend the arm sections of the armature down so they are parallel with the sides of the t-shirt.

6 To make the arms, roll two 5g (<¼oz) balls of brown modelling paste into 7.5cm (3") long sausages. Thin each sausage 1cm (³⁄₈") from the end to form the wrists. Flatten the paste beyond the wrist into a disc. Use a craft knife to cut away a small triangle from each hand to create the thumbs (H). Roll the thumbs between your fingers to round off the edges. Lightly stretch the piece of paste where the fingers will be then cut into it three times to create the fingers. Round off the cut edges, as before. Bend the hands at the wrists.

7 Dip the end of a 12.5cm (5") section of the armature in edible glue. Feed the first arm along the wire until the top meets the body. The wire should protrude from the palm of the hand. Repeat to add the second arm then shape the upper arms to fit against the body (I).

8 Roll two pea-sized balls of purple Cocoform into ovoids. Flatten the ovoids then fit one around the top of each arm to form the sleeves. Use a

Dresden tool to blend the Cocoform at the seams and add a few creases. Trim the wire so that it finishes 4mm (³⁄₁₆") below the hands.

9 Roll a large-pea-sized ball of brown modelling paste into a cylinder. Glue the cylinder over the neck of the armature. Roll a thin sausage of purple Cocoform and wrap it around the base of the neck.

10 To make the head, roll 25g (>¾oz) of brown modelling paste into an egg shape. Use the side of your hand to lightly indent a groove halfway up the egg. Use your fingers to smooth out any harsh edges. Place your index fingers into the groove on the face, leaving a small gap between them for the bridge of the nose, and lightly press down. Further indent the eye area with a ball tool (J).

11 To make the eye sockets, push the broad end of a Dresden tool into the paste and gently rock from side to side and upwards to open up the eye socket (K). Fill each eye socket with a small piece of white modelling paste.

12 Roll a small ball of brown modelling paste into a capsule shape and glue it in the centre of the face on the lower edge of the groove.

13 Use a Dresden tool to mark in the mouth. Add a dimple at each end using a mini ball tool.

14 For the ears, use a ball tool to create an indentation in each side of the head. Roll two small cones of brown modelling paste and glue them in place in the holes. Push a ball tool into the centre of each ear to create the shape (L).

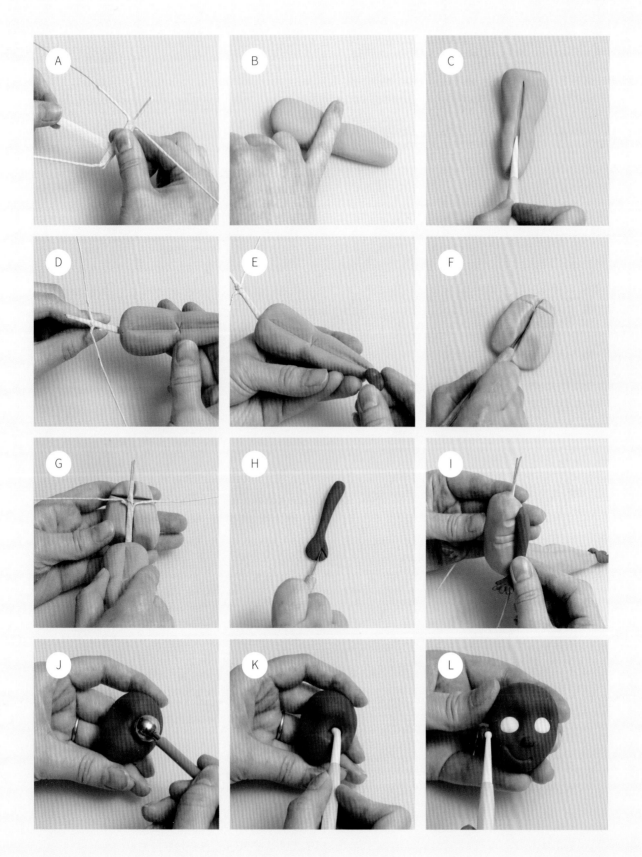

15 Push a 5mm (¼") ball tool into the right side of each eye. Fill the wells with small balls of a 50:50 mix of brown and white modelling paste. Use a smaller ball tool to make a well in each eye for the pupils then fill them with small balls of black modelling paste. Add two tiny balls of white modelling paste to the eyes to form highlights. Glue a very small tapered sausage of black modelling paste along the top of the eye for the eyelashes. Roll two very small tapered sausages of black modelling paste for the eyebrows and glue them in place on the face.

16 Glue the head on to the neck. Shape 15g (½oz) of black modelling paste to fit the back of the head; the paste should reach from ear to ear and to the top of the head. Draw hair lines in the paste with a Dresden tool then glue it in place. Fix a small cone of black modelling paste in front of each ear. For the fringe, divide 5g (<¼oz) of black modelling paste in half, roll them into elongated cone shapes and flatten them slightly. Draw hair lines in the fringe then glue them in place. Add two elongated cones to the front of the hairline. Roll a marble-sized ball of black modelling paste into an elongated cone and use a Dresden tool to mark lines along its length. Starting from the wide end, begin to curl the paste in and around to form a spiral. Glue the bun in place on top of the head.

LOTUS LADY

1 Knead together 30g (1oz) of blue modelling paste and 85g (2¾oz) of white modelling paste. Roll 55g (2oz) of the pale blue paste into a 21cm (8⅜") long sausage shape

with tapered ends and a thicker centre. Bend the sausage in half to form the legs. Bend the paste halfway along each leg to form the knees (M). Trim the ends of both legs straight then bend each one towards the opposite thigh (N). Use a Dresden tool to mark creases around the inner knee and a seam around the centre. Glue the legs on top of your chosen cake.

2 To make the feet, roll a small piece of beige modelling paste into a 1.5cm (½") long sausage. Gently pinch one end to thin and shape the toe area. Roll five tiny balls of beige modelling paste, decreasing in size, and glue them in place on the toe area (O). Repeat to make a second foot then glue them both upside-down, at the ends of the legs (P).

3 Roll 45g (1½oz) of pale blue modelling paste into an egg and flatten the base. Use the side of your little finger to create a groove halfway up the shape (Q). Use your fingers to accentuate the bust and stomach.

4 Knead 5g (<¼oz) of white modelling paste into the same amount of turquoise modelling paste. Shape 5g (<¼oz) of the pale turquoise paste into a disc large enough to cover the base of the egg. Glue the disc in place then use a Dresden tool to mark vertical lines all the way around the edge (R). Push a cocktail stick through the centre of the legs. Gently push the body down over the cocktail stick (S).

5 Divide 15g (½oz) of pale blue modelling paste in half. Roll each piece into a 7cm (2¾") long sausage and bend each one at the halfway point to create the arms. Trim one end of each arm at an angle and the other straight. For the cuffs, add a small disc

of pale turquoise paste to the straight end of each arm and draw vertical lines around the edge, as with the body. Glue the angled end of each arm to the shoulder area of the body and attach the cuffs to the middle of the chest.

6 Repeat the method from step 6 of the Cobra Pose instructions to create two hands using marble-sized balls of beige modelling paste. Glue the hands together at the palms then glue the backs of the hands inside the pale blue cuffs.

7 Roll a pea-sized ball of beige modelling paste into a disc and glue it on top of the body. Wrap a thin sausage of pale turquoise modelling paste around the join and mark vertical lines in the edge using a Dresden tool.

8 Repeat step 10 from the Cobra Pose instructions using 25g (>¾oz) of beige modelling paste to make the head. Roll a pea-sized ball

of beige modelling paste into a cone. Glue the cone to the centre of the face with the pointed end over the bridge of the nose. Use a silicone-tipped tool to blend the join and shape the nose (T). Push a small ball tool into the base of the nose to create the nostrils.

9 Repeat steps 13–15 from the Cobra Pose instructions to add the mouth, ears and eyes, omitting the eyebrows. Add two small balls of pale turquoise paste to the earlobes for earrings.

10 Knead a small ball of black modelling paste into 50g (1¾oz) of white modelling paste to make a grey paste. Roll two small pieces of the grey paste into cone shapes and fix them above the eyes. Add texture using a Dresden tool. Glue a small cone of grey paste in front of each ear.

11 Divide 25g (>¾oz) of the grey modelling paste into 12 balls: two large, three medium and seven small. Glue the two large balls together. Glue the three medium balls together in a horizontal line and glue them beneath the two large ones. Glue three of the small balls in a horizontal line above the two large ones then add two underneath the first row. Glue the remaining two on either side of the two large ones. Roll out a piece of grey modelling paste into a thin sheet. Glue the sheet over the cluster of balls and tuck the edges underneath. Glue the arrangement to the back of the head.

12 Divide 15g (½oz) of grey modelling paste into five balls and roll them into cone shapes. Starting from the wide end, curl the paste in and around to form a spiral (U). Lightly flatten the spirals and glue them around the hairline.

DOG

1 Knead Teddy Bear Brown paste food colour into 35g (1¼oz) of white modelling paste to make a golden brown colour. Roll 20g (¾oz) of golden brown paste into an egg. Lightly grease your fingers with white vegetable fat and begin gently pinching and pulling the paste at the wider end to extrude two short back legs. Repeat to form two front legs at the opposite end of the egg (V). The front legs should be 1cm (⅜") long.

2 Use your fingers to bend the chest upwards and fold the front legs down to bear the weight of the chest (W). Use a Dresden tool to mark folds in the skin under the front legs and between the back legs. Lightly pinch the tip of the front legs to form a small foot and use a Dresden tool to mark in the toes. Glue a small cone of paste to the base of the back for the tail.

3 To make the head, roll 10g (¼oz) of golden brown paste into a ball. Use your little finger to lightly indent a groove just above the midline on the ball (X). Gently ease out the paste at the wider end to give a more pronounced muzzle (Y). Use a Dresden tool to draw a mouth on the muzzle (Z). Push the wider end of the Dresden tool into the centre of the mouth and gently push down towards to open it up (AA). Use a mini ball tool or cocktail stick to indent a small hole at either end of the smile and three small holes on each cheek. Insert a small cone of pink modelling paste into the open mouth and use a Dresden tool to draw a line down the centre of the tongue. Add a small ovoid of black modelling paste to the face for the nose.

4 Lightly press the wider end of a ball tool into the face on either side of the nose then use your fingers to smooth away the edges of the indentation. Use a 5mm (¼") ball tool to indent the eye sockets. Fill the eye sockets with two small balls of white modelling paste. Use a black food colour pen to mark in the pupils.

5 For the ears, roll two small balls of golden brown modelling paste into cones. Flatten the cones slightly then press a bulbous cone tool into the centre of each cone to create the ears. Glue the ears on top of the dog's head.

6 Shape a marble-sized ball of pink modelling paste into a disc. Glue the disc to the dog's neck then glue the head on top of the disc.

MAKE THE CAKE

COVERING

1 Use 650g (1lb 7oz) of Iced Mint sugarpaste to cover the 33cm (13") cake drum (see page 30).

2 Use 750g (1lb 10½oz) of Iced Mint sugarpaste to cover the 18cm (7") cake and 500g (1lb 1¾oz) of Iced Mint sugarpaste to cover the 12.5cm (5") cake (see page 28). Set the covered cakes and drum aside to firm for 24 hours.

3 Knead ½tsp of CMC into the remaining Iced Mint sugarpaste. Wrap the paste well and set it aside for two hours.

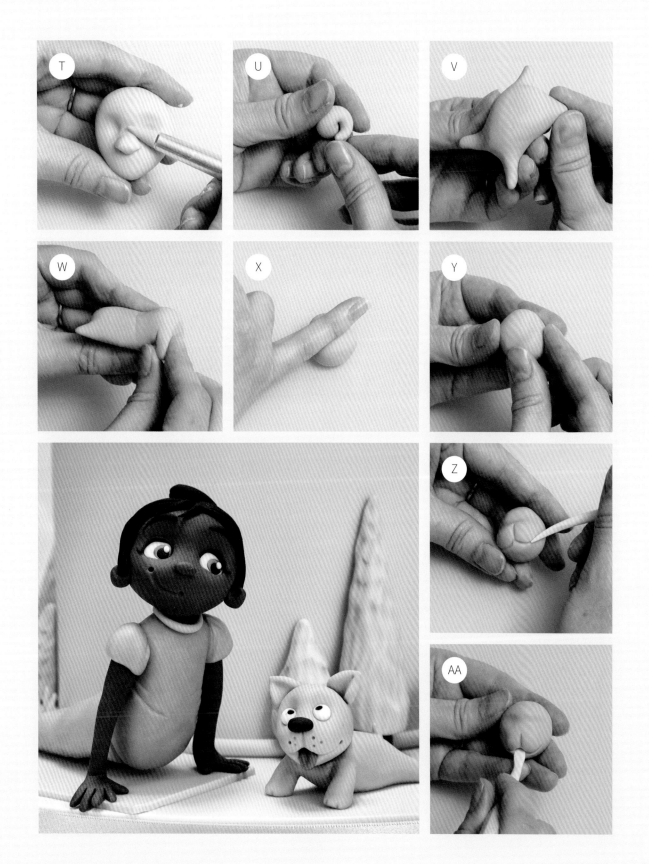

4   Once the sugarpaste on the cakes is firm, dowel and stack them (see page 31). Allow the royal icing to dry for one hour.

5   Roll the CMC-strengthened Iced Mint sugarpaste into a sausage shape 5mm (¼") in diameter and 59cm (23") long. Use edible glue to fix the sausage of paste around the base of the 18cm (7") cake. Repeat to add a 42cm (16½") sausage around the base of the 12.5cm (5") cake.

6   Use double-sided tape to fix Iced Mint ribbon around the edge of the drum.

SIGNPOST

1   Knead together 20g (¾oz) of Brown modelling paste and 20g (¾oz) of White SFP. Roll out the paste to a 1mm (<¹⁄₁₆") thickness and cut out an 11cm x 4cm (4¼" x 1½") rectangle. Cut away small rectangles from either end to create a wooden plank effect. Use a Dresden tool to mark in the planks and woodgrain (AB).

2   Roll the remaining paste into two 5mm (¼") diameter (4") long sausages. Use the Dresden tool to mark in the woodgrain using varying

pressures. Trim the base of the sausage to a flat edge. Set the pieces aside to firm for one hour.

3   Roll out 25g (>¾oz) of Black SFP into a thin sheet. Lightly grease the surface of the paste with a little white vegetable fat. Cut out the wording 'Namaste' using the letter cutters. Glue the letters on the sign.

4   Use edible glue to fix the sign post to the front of the 12.5cm (5") cake.

TREES AND BUSHES

1   Knead a little Sunny Lime paste food colour into the remaining strengthened Iced Mint sugarpaste. Divide the paste into three 10g (¼oz) balls, three 15g (½oz) balls and two 35g (1¼oz) balls. Roll each ball into a cone then flatten the backs. Starting at the bottom edge and working towards the point, use a Dresden tool to create dimples in the cones' surface (AC).

2   Roll eight 15g (½oz) pieces of brown modelling paste into cylinders approximately 1cm (³⁄₈") tall. Use a Dresden tool to mark a woodgrain texture in the surface of each cylinder. Glue one cylinder to

the base of each cone then attach the trees around the base of each tier using edible glue.

3   Roll 90g (3oz) of the strengthened sugarpaste into 20 balls of various sizes. Clump the balls together into three bush shapes, starting with the largest balls in the centre and working out to the smaller balls around the edges (AD).

4   Roll out the remaining strengthened sugarpaste into a thin sheet. Paint a thin layer of edible glue over the surface of each bush and lay the paste over the top. Use your fingers to work the paste around the balls (AE). Trim away any excess and then turn the bush over and fold the remaining paste underneath. Glue two of the bushes to the drum and the third around the base of the signpost.

5   Roll the remaining strengthened sugarpaste into small cones and glue them around the edges of the cake and drum in clusters of three.

YOGA MATS

1   Knead together 20g (¾oz) of white modelling paste and 20g (¾oz) of yellow modelling paste. Roll out the pale yellow paste to a 2mm (¹⁄₁₆") thickness.

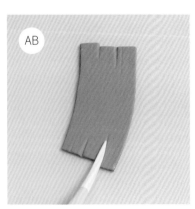

AB

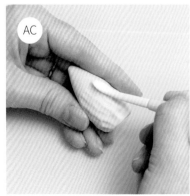

AC

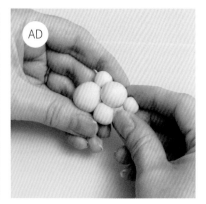

AD

Cut out an 11.5cm x 6.5cm (4½" x 2½") rectangle and fix it to the left side of the front of the drum.

2 Make a second rectangle using a mixture of 30g (1oz) of white modelling paste and 10g (¼oz) of pink modelling paste. Roll the rectangle up tightly. Roll out 5g (<¼oz) of pink modelling paste into a thin sheet and cut out a 5mm x 10cm (¼" x 4") strip. Cut the strip in half and glue one piece around each end of the rolled-up mat. For the handle, cut a 5mm x 4cm (¼" x 1½") strip and glue it between the two bands. Glue the pink yoga mat towards the right side of the front of the drum.

MODELS

1 Use edible glue to fix the Cobra Pose figure on top of the yellow mat on the drum. Glue the dog in front of the figure so they are looking at each other.

2 Build the Lotus Lady on top of the top tier of the cake as instructed.

RUCKSACK

1 Knead together 10g (¼oz) of turquoise modelling paste and 15g

(½oz) of white modelling paste. Roll 20g (¾oz) of the pale turquoise paste into an egg shape. Flatten the base and one side of the egg (AF). Use a Dresden tool to mark a line from the base, across the top and down to the other side (AG). Mark a crease halfway up the bag on each side.

2 Roll a pea-sized ball of the pale turquoise paste into a short sausage shape. Flatten the sausage slightly and glue it to front of the bag. Mark a crease on the front.

3 Combine a marble-sized ball of pale turquoise paste with the same amount of White. Roll the paste out into a thin sheet and cut out a 3mm (⅛") wide strip. Use a Dresden tool to mark V shapes and a central line along the length of the strip. Cut off a 4cm (1½") length and glue it over the top and sides of the bag. Cut a small piece and glue it over the front pocket.

4 Roll two tiny cones of pale turquoise paste and flatten them with your fingers. Push a cocktail stick though the wide end of each shape. Glue the zippers in place.

5 Roll the paste out to a 1mm (<¹/₁₆") thickness and cut out

a 5mm x 11.5cm (¼" x 4½") strip. Cut the strip in half to make two straps and glue them to the back of the rucksack. To finish, add a small piece of paste bent into a curve to the top of the bag. Glue the rucksack to the drum positioning it between the dog and the pink yoga mat.

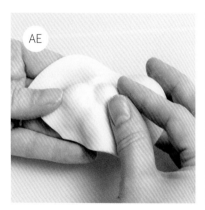

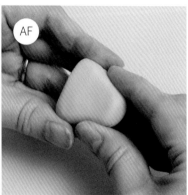

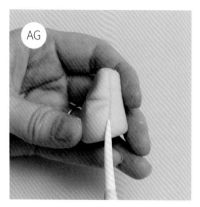

FOREST FAIRY

Add a sprinkling of fairy dust to your party with this fun celebration cake featuring simple but effective cake carving and modelling.

FAIRY MODEL

SK Sugarpaste: 35g (1¼oz) Glamour Red, 50g (1¾oz) Mocha Cream

SK Sugar Florist Paste (SFP): 85g (2¾oz) White

Polystyrene ball: 7.5cm (3")

Clear piping gel

SK HD Sugar Modelling Paste: SK HD Sugar Modelling Paste: 30g (1oz) Beige, <1g (¹/₈oz) Black, 25g (>¾oz) Green, <1g (¹/₈oz) Turquoise, 78g (2¾oz) White and 15g (½oz) Yellow

Round cutters: 6mm, 8mm, 1cm, 1.5cm and 2cm (¼", >¼", ³/₈", ½" and ¾")

SK Great Impressions Butterfly Mould: Large

SK Designer Fairy Sparkle Dust Food Colour: Primrose

SK Designer Dust Food Colour: Pastel Pink

TOADSTOOL CAKE

Round cake drum: 30.5cm (12")

SK Sugarpaste: 600g (1lb 5¼oz) Bridal White, 385g (13½oz) Glamour Red, 600g (1lb 5¼oz) Iced Mint and 235g (8¼oz) Mocha Cream

500g (1lb 1¾oz) buttercream

Round cake cards: 12.5cm and 20.5cm (5" and 8")

Round, filled sponge cake, 12.5cm (5") deep: 18cm (7")

Hemisphere sponge cake, 10cm (4") deep: 20.5cm (8")

SK Bellissimo Flexi Smoothers: Medium

Round cutters: 6mm, 8mm, 1cm, 1.5cm, 2cm, 3cm, 3.5cm, 4cm, 5cm, 7.5cm (¼", >¼", ³/₈", ½", ¾", 1¹/₈", 1³/₈", 1½", 2" and 3")

CMC cellulose gum

SK HD Sugar Modelling Paste: 30g (1oz) Beige, 5g (<¼oz) Black, 15g (½oz) Brown, 25g (>¾oz) Green, 5g (<¼oz) Pink, 10g (¼oz) Turquoise, 185g (6½oz) White and 15g (½oz) Yellow

SK Sugar Florist Paste (SFP): 130g (4½oz) White

SK Designer Paste Food Colour: Sunny Lime

SK Modelling Cocoform: 10g (¼oz) White

Food colour pens: black and orange

FMM Daisy Plunger Cutters: 1.3cm and 2cm (½" and ¾")

Silicone-tipped tool

1.5cm (½") width satin ribbon: 1m (1yd 3³/₈") green

TOADSTOOL

1 Knead together 50g (1¾oz) of Mocha Cream sugarpaste and 50g (1¾oz) of White SFP then add a pinch of CMC. Roll the paste into an egg shape. Use a Dresden tool to draw fine vertical lines from the top and bottom of the shape (A). Push a wooden barbecue skewer through the centre of the stalk then set it aside to firm for 24 hours.

2 Use a serrated knife to cut the 7.5cm (3") polystyrene ball in half. Paint a thin layer of piping gel over the base of the dome. Roll out 30g (1oz) of white modelling paste and cut out a 7.5cm (3") disc. Stick the disc to the base of the dome then use a Dresden tool to draw fine lines radiating out from the centre of the disc to the edge, and from the edge in towards the centre (B). Set the dome aside to firm for 12 hours.

3 Knead together 35g (1¼oz) of Glamour Red sugarpaste and 35g (1¼oz) of White SFP then add a pinch of CMC. Roll out the mixed red paste to a 3mm (⅛") thickness. Paint a thin layer of piping gel over the dome. Lay the paste over the surface of the dome and use your hands to shape the paste around it. Trim away the excess and smooth the cut edge with your fingers.

4 Roll out 15g (½oz) of white modelling paste into a thin sheet. Cut out a variety of discs using the 6mm–2cm (¼"–¾") round cutters and glue them randomly over the toadstool cap.

5 Feed the toadstool cap down over the barbecue skewer and use edible glue to fix it in place.

FAIRY

1 Knead together 25g (>¾oz) of green modelling paste and 25g (>¾oz) of white modelling paste. Roll 30g (1oz) of the pale green paste into an egg. Flatten the base of the egg shape and thread it down over the barbecue skewer in the centre of the toadstool. Use edible glue to fix the body in place. Use a Dresden tool to draw creases in the sides of the body.

2 Knead together 30g (1oz) of beige and 15g (½oz) of white modelling paste. Divide 10g (¼oz) of the light beige modelling paste in half and roll each piece into a 5.5cm (2¼") long sausage shape. Thin the sausages 1cm (³⁄₈") from the end of each piece to form the ankles. Gently pinch the paste just below the ankle so that it sits at a 90° angle from the rest of the leg (C). Use your fingers to shape the paste into a foot then use a craft knife to separate the toes (D). Shape the top of each leg so that they fit against the body. Glue the left leg hanging straight down. Bend the right leg at the knee and glue it to the top of the toadstool (E).

3 Knead 20g (¾oz) of white modelling paste into the remaining pale green modelling paste. Divide 20g (¾oz) of the paste into 10 evenly sized balls. Roll each ball into a cone then flatten each one into a leaf shape. Use a Dresden tool to draw veins on each leaf. Glue the leaves around the bottom of the body, covering the tops of the legs (F).

4 Divide 6g (¼oz) of light beige modelling paste in half. Roll each piece into a 5cm (2") long sausage shape. Thin the sausages 1cm (³⁄₈")

from the end to form the wrists. Gently flatten the paste beyond the wrists into a disc to make the hand (G). Use a craft knife to cut away a small triangle from each hand to create the thumb (H). Roll the thumb between your fingers to round off the edges. Lightly stretch the piece of paste where the fingers will be. Cut into the paste three times to create the fingers and round off the edges. Glue the left arm to the shoulder with the hand resting on the toadstool (I). Bend the right arm at the elbow and attach it with the hand resting in the lap.

5 Divide 5g (<¼oz) of the palest green modelling paste into eight evenly sized balls. Roll each ball into a 2cm (¾") long teardrop shape. Glue four teardrops over each shoulder to make the sleeves (J).

6 Roll a pea-sized ball of light beige modelling paste into a cylinder and push it over the skewer to make the neck. Roll a thin sausage of the palest green modelling paste and glue it around the base of the neck to hide the join (K).

7 Lightly dust the Butterfly mould with cornflour. Press 10g (¼oz) of White Cocoform into the mould and level off the back with a palette knife. Chill the mould for five minutes then turn out the shape (L). Brush the front and back of the wings with Primrose dust food colour. Bend the wings slightly in the middle and attach them to the fairy's back using a little royal icing.

8 For the head, roll 25g (>¾oz) of light beige modelling paste into a teardrop shape. Use the side of your hand to create a groove halfway up the egg. Use your fingers to smooth out the groove and remove any harsh

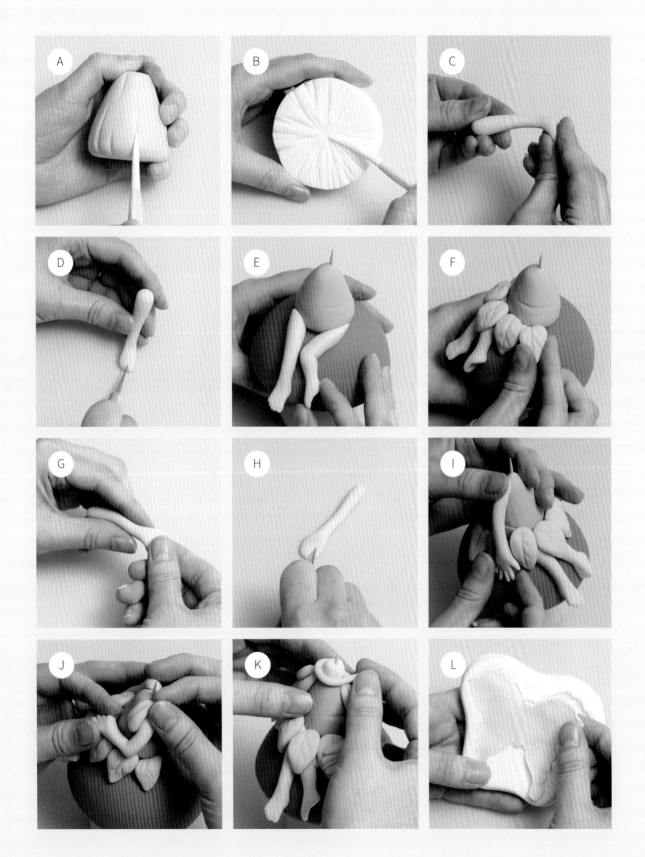

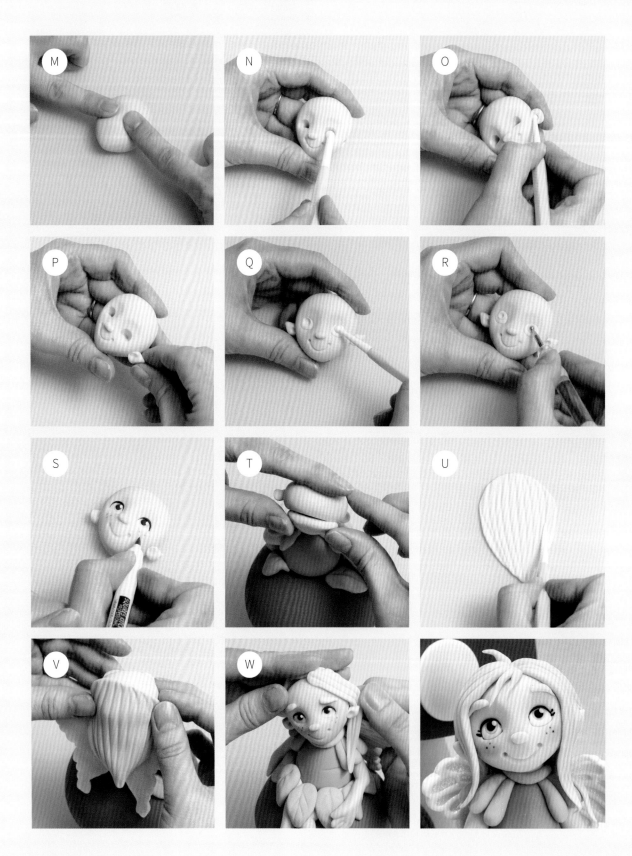

edges. Place your index fingers into the groove on the face, leaving a small gap between them for the bridge of the nose, and lightly press down (M).

9 Roll a small ball of light beige modelling paste into a capsule shape. Glue the nose in the centre of the face, positioning it on the lower edge of the groove. Use a Dresden tool to draw a shallow U shape for the mouth, then use a small ball tool to add a dimple at each end.

10 To make the eye sockets, push a Dresden tool into the wells in the face and gently rock it side to side and upwards to open up the sockets (N).

11 Push the end of a ball tool into each side of the head in line with the nose. Roll two small pieces of light beige paste into cone shapes and glue one into each hole to form the ears. Push a ball tool into the centre of each ear (O). Use your fingers to pinch the tips of the ears to a point (P).

12 Fill each eye socket with a small ball of white modelling paste. Push a ball tool into the top edge of each eye to form a well (Q). Fill the well with a small ball of pale turquoise modelling paste. Use a smaller ball tool to create a small well in the centre of the turquoise circle (R). Fill this with a small ball of black modelling paste. Add two tiny dots of white modelling paste to each eye to form highlights. Roll two pieces of black modelling paste into very small, fine sausage shapes with tapered ends. Glue the eyelashes around the upper edge of each eye.

13 Lightly dust the cheeks with Pastel Pink dust food colour then add three small dots to each

cheek using an orange food colour pen (S). Use a black food colour pen to draw two fine lines at the end of each eye to represent eyelashes.

14 Knead 15g (½oz) of white modelling paste into 15g (½oz) of yellow modelling paste to lighten the colour. Roll two tiny pieces of the pale yellow paste into tapered sausages for the eyebrows and fix them in place on the face using edible glue.

15 Press the head down onto the wooden barbecue skewer and attach it to the neck using edible glue.

16 Shape a small piece of pale yellow modelling paste into a dome and fix it to the back of the head to make it round (T). Roll out 15g (½oz) of pale yellow modelling paste to a 2mm (¹/₁₆") thickness. Cut out a

teardrop shape 8cm long and 5cm wide (3¹/₈" x 2"). Use a Dresden tool to drawn lines down the length of the paste to represent strands of hair (U). Glue the paste to the back of the head, making sure the hair completely covers the top, back and sides (V).

17 Set aside a small ball of pale yellow modelling paste to use for loose strands of hair. Divide the remaining paste into quarters and roll each piece into a long teardrop shape. Flatten the teardrops with a rolling pin then draw lines in the surface with a Dresden tool. Glue two teardrops to each side of the head (W).

18 Divide the remaining pale yellow modelling paste into three teardrop shapes. Fix one piece at the crown and the remaining two at the hairline.

SHAPING AND COVERING

1 Cover the cake drum using 600g (1lb 5¼oz) of Iced Mint sugarpaste (see page 30).

2 Spread a small amount of buttercream onto the 12.5cm (5") cake card and place the 18cm (7") filled cake centrally on top. Place the second 12.5cm (5") cake card centrally on top of the cake. Use a serrated knife to trim the cake so that the bottom and top of the cake match the two cake cards. The cake should be at its widest 4cm (1½") from the base, measuring approximately 16.5cm (6½") in diameter. Remove the 12.5cm (5") cake card from the top of the cake.

3 Spread a little buttercream onto the 20.5cm (8") cake board and place the 20.5cm (8") hemisphere cake on top.

4 Spread a thin layer of buttercream over the surface of both cakes, using a Flexi Smoother to ensure it's smooth and even. Refrigerate the cakes for approximately four hours before covering.

5 Brush the hemisphere cake with a little cooled, boiled water. Knead together 300g (10½oz) of Glamour Red sugarpaste and 300g (10½oz) of Bridal White sugarpaste. Roll out the sugarpaste to a 4mm (³/₁₆") thickness and lay it over the cake, using your hands to smooth the surface. Trim away most of the excess paste, leaving a 1cm (³/₈") border around the edge

of the cake. Place the cake on top of a small support, such as a 15cm (6") cake tin, and carefully fold the excess paste underneath the cake drum, fixing it in place with a little piping gel. Smooth the sugarpaste around the curved shape and create a neat finish.

6 Knead 150g (5¼oz) of Mocha Cream sugarpaste into 300g (10½oz) of Bridal White sugarpaste. Roll out the mixed sugarpaste to a 4mm (³/₁₆") thickness. Brush the carved, cylindrical cake with a little cooled, boiled water and lay the sugarpaste over the top. Smooth the sugarpaste around the curved shape then trim away the excess around the base. Use a Dresden tool to draw fine vertical lines from the top and bottom of the cake. Set the cakes and drum aside to firm for 24 hours.

ASSEMBLY

1 Use royal icing to fix the carved cylindrical cake towards the back left side of the covered cake drum. Insert three evenly spaced cake dowels into the top of the cake and trim them to size (see page 31).

2 Spread the remaining royal icing over the dowelled area and place the 20.5cm (8") cake on top. Gently press down to adhere.

DECORATION

1 Use a 3.5cm (1³/₈") round cutter to cut away two discs of sugarpaste 6cm (2³/₈") up from the base of the cylindrical cake and 5cm (2") apart for the windows.

2 Knead 5g (<¼oz) of turquoise modelling paste into 15g (½oz) of white modelling paste. Roll out the pale turquoise paste to a 4mm (³/₁₆") thickness and cut out two discs using the 3.5cm (1³/₈") round cutter. Attach the discs of paste inside the round holes on the cake.

3 Use the 5cm (2") round cutter to cut out a door shape from the space between the two turquoise circles. To create the shape, press one side of the cutter into the cake, applying pressure from the outer edge of the circle down towards the base of the cake, then repeat on the other side.

4   Combine 5g (<¼oz) of pink, 5g (<¼oz) of turquoise and 10g (¼oz) of white modelling paste to create a lilac colour. Roll out the lilac paste to a 4mm (³/₁₆") thickness. Use the 5cm (2") round cutter to cut out a matching door shape to replace the section which has been removed. Fix the door in place using edible glue. Use a Dresden tool to draw four vertical lines in the door then add faint lines to represent woodgrain.

5   Knead together 25g (>¾oz) of White SFP and 15g (½oz) of brown modelling paste. Roll out the brown paste into a thin sheet and cut out four squares, leaving a 5mm (¼") gap between them to make a cross shape (X). Position the 3.5cm (1³/₈") round cutter over the centre of the cross and cut away the excess (Y). Repeat to create a second cross. Use the pointed end of a Dresden tool to add a wood grain texture to the surface of each cross (Z). Use edible glue to fix one cross over each window.

6   Roll out a little more of the mixed brown paste and cut out two discs using the 4cm (1½") round cutter. Cut away the centre of each disc using the 3cm (1¹/₈") round cutter. Add the woodgrain texture, as before, then glue them around the edges of the windows (AA).

7   Roll out the remaining mixed brown paste and cut out a 5mm x 15cm (¼" x 6") strip. Add the woodgrain texture then glue the strip in place around the door (AB). Trim away any excess with a sharp knife. Roll a pea-sized ball of the mixed brown paste and glue it on the right side of the door for the handle.

MINI TOADSTOOLS

1   Knead together 35g (1¼oz) of Mocha Cream sugarpaste and 35g (1¼oz) of White SFP, then add a pinch of CMC. Divide the paste into two portions of 50g and 20g (1¾oz and ¾oz). Roll each ball into an egg shape. Use a Dresden tool to draw fine vertical lines from the top and bottom of each shape. Set the stalks aside to firm for 24 hours.

2   Knead together 50g (1¾oz) of Glamour Red sugarpaste and 50g (1¾oz) of White SFP, then add ¼tsp of CMC. Divide the paste into one 70g (2½oz) ball and one 30g (1oz) ball. Shape each ball into a dome and set them aside to firm for 24 hours.

3   Roll out 15g (½oz) of white modelling paste into a thin sheet. Cut out a variety of discs using the 6mm–2cm (¼"–¾") round cutters and glue them randomly over both toadstool caps.

4   Use a little royal icing to attach the toadstool stalks to the cake drum, positioning them to the left of the cake. Attach the small and medium caps on top of the corresponding stalks.

5   Push a scribing tool into the right side of the cake drum to create a hole large enough for the wooden barbecue skewer. Insert the wooden skewer at the base of the fairy toadstool into the hole and secure it with a little royal icing. Allow the royal icing to set for 12 hours.

FINISHING TOUCHES

1   Roll out a small amount of white modelling paste into a thin sheet and use the daisy cutters to cut out six small and three medium daisies. Glue a small ball of yellow modelling paste in the centre of each flower. Lay the daisies in a foam drying tray to firm for two hours.

2   Divide 25g (>¾oz) of Mocha Cream sugarpaste into 10 balls of different sizes and gently flatten each ball in the palm of your hand. Attach the balls to the cake drum in a pathway leading from the door to the edge of the drum. Use a Dresden tool and ball tools to add a mottled and cracked texture to the surface of each ball.

3   Knead Sunny Lime paste food colour into 20g (¾oz) of White SFP to make a lime green colour. Divide the paste into approximately 16 balls of different sizes. Roll each ball into an elongated cone shape then bend the tip over into a spiral. Trim the wide end on each piece flat. Use edible glue to fix the cones to the cake drum in groups of two or three. Once firm, add the daisies to the cake drum in the same way.

4   Wrap green ribbon around the edge of the cake drum and secure it with double-sided tape.

CRAZY CATS

These fun characters have plenty of cat-titude. Make the moggies match your own by adapting the colours and markings then create a sweet and simple cake to display them on.

POUNCING CAT

SK HD Sugar Modelling Paste: 120g (4¼oz) White

SK Professional Paste Food Colours: Berberis and Terracotta

UPRIGHT CAT

SK HD Sugar Modelling Paste: 120g (4¼oz) Black and 20g (¾oz) White

SK Sugar Florist Paste (SFP): 15g (½oz) Candy Pink and 5g (<¼oz) Marigold

SLEEPING CAT

SK HD Sugar Modelling Paste: 120g (4¼oz) White

SK Professional Paste Food Colours: Berberis and Terracotta

PME Scallop Tool

MOUSE

SK HD Sugar Modelling Paste: 10g (¼oz) Black and 20g (¾) White

SK Sugar Florist Paste (SFP): 5g (<¼oz) Candy Pink

CAKE

SK Sugarpaste: 2kg (4lb 6½oz) Dove Grey

Round cake drum: 30.5cm (12")

Round, filled sponge cakes, 12.5cm (5") deep: 12.5cm and 18cm (5" and 7")

Round cake boards: 12.5cm and 18cm (5" and 7")

650g (1lb 7oz) buttercream

1.5cm (½") width double-faced satin ribbon: 1m (1yd 3⅜") grey

½tsp CMC cellulose gum

Round cutter: 4cm (1½")

SK Sugar Florist Paste (SFP): 10g (¼oz) Candy Blue, 20g (¾oz) Candy Pink, 20g (¾oz) Marigold and 60g (2oz) White

SK HD Sugar Modelling Paste: 5g (<¼oz) Black

Floral wire: 26-gauge white

PME Blossom Cutters: 1.3cm and 2.5cm (½" and 1")

FMM Multi-flower Veiner

SK Great Impressions Feather Mould: 5cm (2")

SK Designer Pastel Dust Food Colour: Soft Green

Floral tape: white

Posy picks: 2 x small

POUNCING CAT

1   Roll 65g (2¼oz) of white modelling paste into an egg shape and place it on its side. Colour 10g (¼oz) of white modelling paste with Berberis paste food colour. Knead a small amount of white vegetable fat into a large-pea-sized ball of the Berberis-coloured modelling paste to soften it. Gently flatten the ball into a disc and glue it onto the back of the body. Grease your fingers with more white vegetable fat and press the Berberis-coloured modelling paste into the white modelling paste to make a smooth join.

2   Use a silicone-tipped tool to make indentations in the haunches for the back legs (A). Smooth away any harsh lines with your finger. Push a ball tool into the top of the back of the body to make a hole for the tail.

3   To make the tail, roll 4g (<¼oz) of white modelling paste into a tapered sausage. Cut away the wider end and replace it with a cone of Berberis-coloured modelling paste. Blend the seams using your fingers. Bend the tail into an S shape and gently feed a cocktail stick into the wider end (B). Set the tail aside to firm for at least two hours then glue it into the hole in the back of the body.

4   For the back paws, roll two large-pea-sized balls of white modelling paste into cone shapes and use a Dresden tool to mark in the toes (C). Use edible glue to fix the paws underneath the haunches at the back of the body.

5   For the front legs, roll two larger balls of white modelling paste into sausage shapes with a bulge at one end. Slightly flatten the wider ends to make the paws and mark in the toes with a Dresden tool (D). Bend each leg at the halfway point (E). Use edible glue to fix one leg to each side of the body, arranging the left paw so that it is slightly further forwards than the right (F). Rub a little white vegetable fat onto the join and use a silicone-tipped tool to blend the seams. Using the same technique as for the back and tail, add patches of Berberis-coloured modelling paste on the joint in each leg and across the shoulders onto the back.

6   For the head, roll 25g (>¾oz) of white modelling paste into an ovoid and shape the ends to points. Use the side of your finger to mark a groove across the eye area (G). Grease your hands with white vegetable fat and begin shaping the muzzle (H). Add a triangular patch of Berberis-coloured modelling paste over the forehead and down towards the muzzle, blending the edges, as before (I).

7   Push a large ball tool into the face on either side of the muzzle (J). Blend out the harsh lines with your fingers. Push a 6mm (¼") ball tool into either side of the face to create the eye sockets (K). The holes created should be around 4mm (³/₁₆") deep.

8   Thin out the points on the outer edges of the face then divide them in two using a Dresden tool. Use your fingers to refine the points. Draw in the mouth with the pointed end of a Dresden tool then use the broader end to push the paste away from the lower jaw, creating the chin (L). Use a ball tool to gradually push the paste away from the mouth, further accentuating the chin and upper lip. Use a mini ball tool to mark in the holes for the whiskers.

9   Roll two small balls of white modelling paste and glue them into the eye sockets. Push the small end of a ball tool into each eye at the inner edge and fill the holes with small balls of Bow Tie Black modelling paste. Add a tiny dot of white paste to the pupil for a highlight.

10   For the nose, colour a very small piece of white modelling paste deep orange using Terracotta paste food colour. Shape the deep orange modelling paste into a triangle and fix it to the face using edible glue.

11   For the ears, roll two pea-sized balls of white modelling paste and two pea-sized balls of Berberis-coloured modelling paste into cone shapes. Cut away the top of one of the white cones and replace it with the piece of Berberis-coloured modelling paste of the same size. For the other ear, cut away one side of the white cone and replace it with the matching Berberis-coloured modelling paste. Blend the seams then flatten the cones between your fingers. Use a Dresden tool to shape the inner ears (M). Glue the ears on top of the head.

12   Glue three very fine strips of Terracotta-coloured modelling paste to the top of the head, between the ears. Glue the head to the body.

UPRIGHT CAT

1   Roll 65g (2¼oz) of black modelling paste into a cone. Use a silicone-tipped tool to mark in the haunches (N, see page 78). With each stroke, use your fingers to smooth the paste in the middle, leaving the haunches sitting proud.

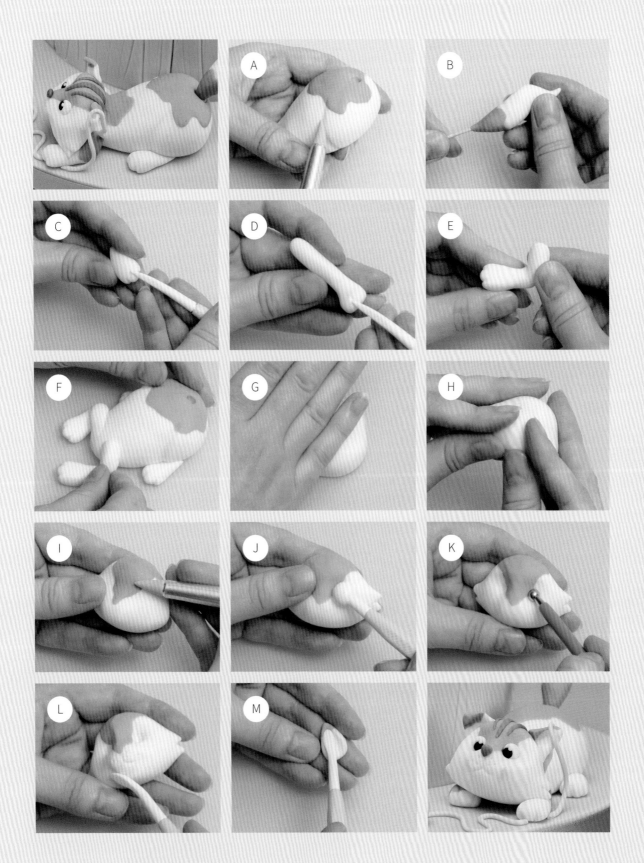

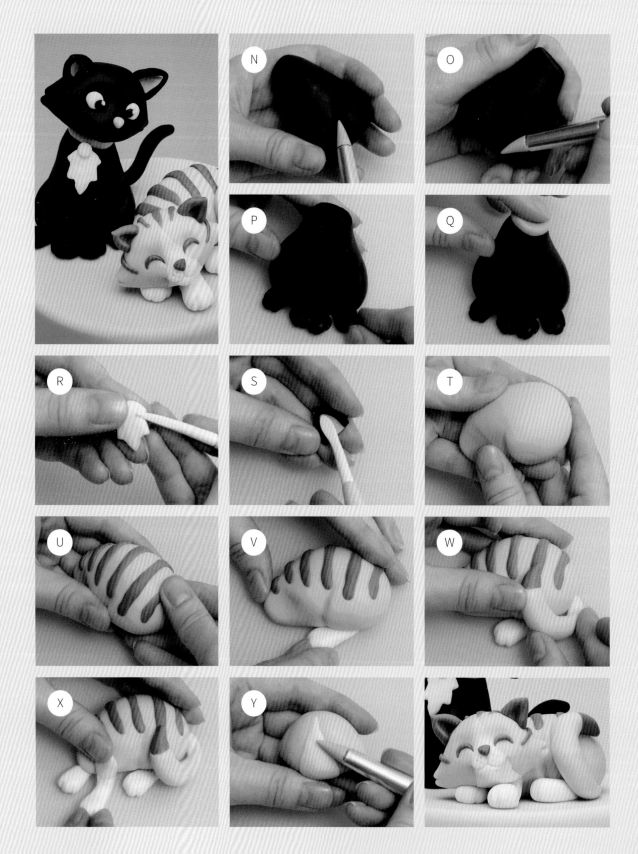

2   Use a silicone-tipped tool to mark the front legs, drawing four lines from the middle of the chest down to the base (O). Smooth down the area on either side of each leg to make the legs stand out from the body. Cut the neck at a slight angle, making it higher on the left side than the right.

3   Flatten two pea-sized balls of black modelling paste for the front paws. Use a Dresden tool to mark in the toes. Glue one paw to the bottom of each front leg. Shape two larger balls of black modelling paste into cones then add toes, as before. Glue the pointed ends underneath the back legs (P).

4   For the tail, roll 3g (<¼oz) of black modelling paste into a thin sausage. Glue the tail to the back of the body and support it with food-grade foam until secure.

5   Flatten a ball of Candy Pink SFP into a thick disc approximately 2cm (¾") in diameter and glue the disc on top of the neck (Q).

6   To make the white patch of fur, roll a pea-sized ball of white modelling paste into a cone and flatten it a little. Push a Dresden tool into the paste twice on each side (R). Use your fingers to shape the edges of the paste into points and fix the patch to the chest using edible glue.

7   Flatten a very tiny ball of Marigold SFP into a disc. Glue the tag to the chest just below the Candy Pink disc. Push a cocktail stick down through the neck and into the body.

8   For the head, repeat steps 6–8 from the Pouncing Cat instructions using 30g (1oz) of black modelling paste.

9   Roll two small balls of white modelling paste and glue them into the eye sockets. Push the small end of a ball tool into the inner edge of each eye and fill each well with a small ball of black modelling paste. Add a tiny dot of white modelling paste to make a highlight.

10   For the nose, shape a very small piece of Candy Pink SFP into a triangle and fix it in place using edible glue.

11   For the ears, shape two small pieces of black modelling paste into cones and make two smaller cones of Candy Pink SFP. Place the pink cones on top of the black cones and gently flatten them to fix the two together. Use a Dresden tool to shape the inner ears (S). Glue the ears on the top of the head.

12   Leave the head and body to firm separately overnight before assembling. Once firm, use edible glue to attach the head to the body.

SLEEPING CAT

1   Colour 80g (2¾oz) of white modelling paste a pale orange colour using Berberis paste food colour. Colour 10g (¼oz) of white modelling paste a burnt orange colour using Terracotta paste food colour.

2   Roll 55g (2oz) of Berberis-coloured modelling paste into an egg shape. Lay the egg on its side and use a silicone-tipped tool to mark in the hind legs (T). Roll small pieces of Terracotta-coloured modelling paste into thin, tapered sausages and use edible glue to fix the stripes across the cat's back (U).

3   Roll a large-pea-sized ball of white modelling paste into a cone and flatten it slightly. Use a Dresden tool to mark in toes then glue the paw underneath the hind leg (V).

4   Shape 5g (<¼oz) of Berberis-coloured modelling paste into a sausage with tapered ends. Trim away the tip at one end and replace it with a cone of Terracotta-coloured modelling paste. Glue the tail to the cat's back and curl it up around the hind leg (W).

5   Use a Dresden tool to mark toes in one side of a pea-sized ball of white modelling paste to make a paw. Fix the paw underneath the neck. Shape a slightly larger piece of white modelling paste into a sausage, leaving one end slightly wider. Lightly flatten the wider end and mark in the toes with the Dresden tool. Replace the other end of the sausage with Berberis-coloured modelling paste. Bend the sausage slightly halfway along its length and glue it to the front of the neck (X).

6   For the head, roll 20g (¾oz) of Berberis-coloured modelling paste into an ovoid and shape the ends to rounded points. Use the side of your finger to mark a groove across the eye area. Shape a piece of white modelling paste into a long triangle and attach it to the face so it runs from the chin to the forehead, smoothing the joins so they blend seamlessly (Y).

7   Lightly grease your hands with white vegetable fat and begin shaping the muzzle. Push the large end of a ball tool into the face on either side of the muzzle then blend out the harsh lines. Thin out the points on the outer edges of the face then divide them in two using a Dresden tool. Use

your fingers to refine the points. Mark in the mouth with a Dresden tool then use the wider end of the tool to push the paste away from the lower jaw, creating the chin. Use a mini ball tool to mark in the holes for the whiskers.

8 Use a scallop tool to mark in the eyes on either side of the nose. Roll two tiny pieces of Terracotta-coloured modelling paste into very fine tapered sausages and fix them over the scallop marks (Z).

9 Shape a small piece of Terracotta-coloured modelling paste into a triangle and fix it on the nose using edible glue.

10 For the ears, roll two pea-sized balls of Terracotta-coloured paste into cone shapes. Use a Dresden tool to shape the inner ears then glue them on top of the head.

11 Roll three tiny pieces of Terracotta-coloured modelling paste into very fine sausages tapered at one end. Fix the stripes so they run from between the ears to the back of the head. Add one stripe to each side of the face in the same way. Fix the head to the body using edible glue.

MOUSE

1 Knead small pinches of black modelling paste into 15g (½oz) of white modelling paste to create a mid-grey tone.

2 Roll 5g (<¼oz) of mid-grey modelling paste into a cone and gently tease the point of the cone

upwards to make the mouse's nose (AA). Use a Dresden tool to draw a smile on the mouse's face and push a very small ball tool into the ends of the smile to make dimples. Push the ball tool gently into the paste on either side of the face to form the eye sockets. Use your fingers to smooth away any harsh lines. Use a small ball tool to mark where the eyes will sit within the eye sockets and where the ears will sit on top of the head (AB).

3 Push a ball tool into the centre of a pea-sized ball of mid-grey modelling paste and pinch one end to a point (AC). Glue the pinched end into one of the holes in the top of the head (AD). Repeat to make and attach a second ear.

4 For the eyes, fill each hole in the face with a small ball of white modelling paste. Use a small ball tool to mark the holes for the pupils and fill them with black modelling paste (AE). Finally, add a tiny dot of white modelling paste to each eye to make a highlight.

5 Glue a tiny oval of Candy Pink SFP onto the tip of the nose.

6 For the body, roll 8g (¼oz) of mid-grey paste into an egg shape. Pinch out two small points from the narrow end of the shape to form the front legs (AF). Trim away the wide end using a sharp knife (AG). Roll two small balls of Candy Pink SFP and flatten them slightly. Use a Dresden tool to mark two lines in the front of each foot. Glue the feet to the legs then glue the head to the body.

COVERING

1 Cover the cake drum using 500g (1lb 1¾oz) of Dove Grey sugarpaste (see page 30).

2 Use 750g (1lb 10½oz) of Dove Grey sugarpaste to cover the 18cm (7") cake and 400g (14oz) of Dove Grey sugarpaste to cover the 12.5cm (5") cake (see page 28). Set the covered cakes and drum aside to firm for 24 hours.

3 Once firm, dowel and stack the cakes (see page 31).

4 Use double-sided tape to fix grey ribbon around the edge of the drum.

WOOD PANELLING

1 Knead ½tsp of CMC into 500g (1lb 1¾oz) of Dove Grey sugarpaste. Wrap the sugarpaste tightly in cling film and set it aside for two hours.

2 Cut out a 7cm x 13.5cm (2¾"x 5¼") rectangular template from a sheet of card.

3 Cut several strips of baking parchment slightly larger than the template and lightly grease them with white vegetable fat. Roll out the strengthened Dove Grey sugarpaste to a 2mm (¹/₁₆") thickness and lay it right-side down on top of the greased

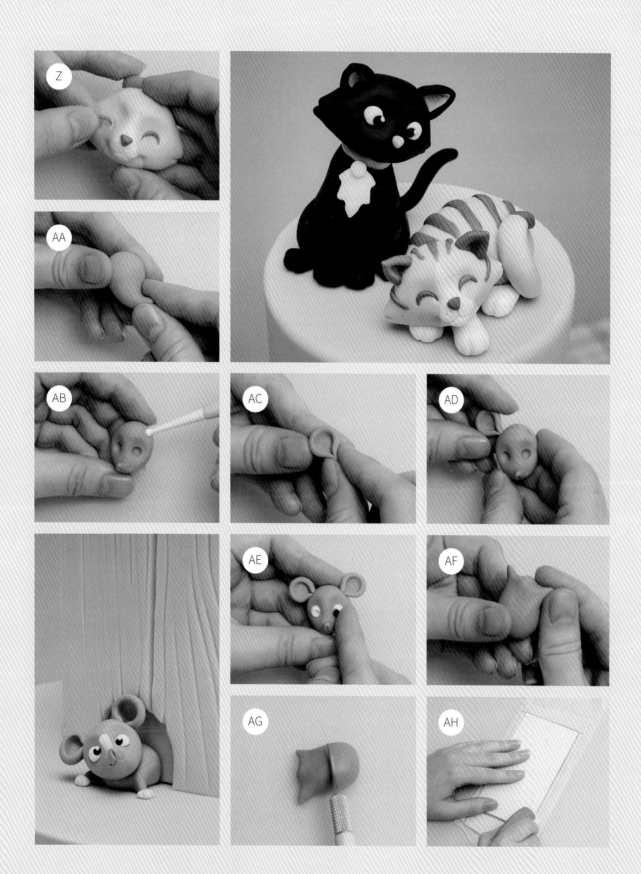

strips. Use the template and a cutting wheel to cut out eight rectangles on individual strips of paper (AH, see page 81). Lay two of the strips next to each other and use a 4cm (1½") round cutter to cut out a semi-circle from the centre (AI).

4 Brush the side of the 18cm (7") cake with edible glue. Carefully lift up a sheet of the baking parchment and use it to attach the sugarpaste strip to the side of the cake (AJ). Use a straight-edged smoother or ruler to straighten the edges. Continue working around the cake until all the strips are in place.

5 Use a Dresden tool to draw a woodgrain pattern on each strip of sugarpaste, varying the length of the lines and adding knots where desired (AK).

LETTERING

1 Knead a pinch of black modelling paste into 10g (¼oz) of White SFP to form a dark grey colour.

2 Cut out a 7cm x 5cm (2¾" x 2") rectangle of baking parchment and draw a 6cm (2⅜") guideline along the bottom edge. Write your chosen name or message on the parchment then turn it over and lightly grease the surface with white vegetable fat.

3 Using the reversed template, start to build the letters using thin sausages of dark grey SFP, cutting and thinning the ends as you go (AL).

4 Once the writing is complete, measure and mark the halfway point along the top of the paper. Use a scribing tool to mark the centre of the front of the 12.5cm (5") cake.

5 Paint a thin layer of edible glue onto the backs of the letters then carefully lift the baking parchment up to the cake. Match the two halfway points and fix the letters in place just below the centre of the cake (AM).

WREATH DECORATION

1 To make the balls of string, combine 15g (½oz) of Candy Pink SFP with the same amount of White SFP. Divide the pale pink paste into two larger balls and one smaller ball. Use a Dresden tool to mark lines running over the surface of the balls (AN). Set the balls aside to firm.

2 For the flower centres, cut ten 26-gauge white floral wires into thirds. Roll a small piece of White SFP into a ball. Dip the end of a piece of wire in edible glue and insert it into the ball, then use your fingers to shape the ball around the wire. Repeat to make a total of 15 flower centres using White SFP, six using Marigold SFP and two using Candy Pink SFP.

3 Roll out a small piece of Candy Pink SFP to a 1mm (<¹/₁₆") thickness. Use the blossom cutters to cut out two 1.3cm (½") flowers and one 2.5cm (1") flower. Place each flower on a foam pad and use a ball tool to soften the edges of the petals. Press the larger flower between the two halves of the multi-flower veiner. Thread a wired ball through the centre of each flower and fix the petals around the edge of the ball using edible glue.

4 Repeat step 3 to make one large and five small blue flowers, two large and four small yellow flowers, two large and two small white flowers and two large and three small flowers

made with a 50:50 mix of Candy Pink and Candy Blue SFP. Set all the flowers aside to firm overnight.

5 For the feathers, roll out 10g (¼oz) of White SFP very finely, leaving a thicker vein of paste running down the centre (AO). Lay the feather mould over the SFP and lightly press down to imprint the pattern (AP). Remove the mould and cut away the excess paste around the edge. Place the shape between the two halves of the mould and press down to imprint the pattern. Use a sharp knife to cut narrow V shapes out of the sides of the feather. Dip the end of a third-length 26-gauge white floral wire in edible glue and feed it through the central vein until it reaches two thirds of the way up the feather. Repeat this step to make six wired feathers. Leave the feathers to firm on a foam pad overnight, laying them over scrunched up kitchen paper to create movement. Lightly dust the bases of the feathers with Soft Green dust food colour.

6 Tape the flowers and leaves into two curved sprays using half-width white floral tape. Start each spray with a feather at the top then add flowers and more feathers along the wire. Trim the end of each spray and insert them into small posy picks. Push the posy picks into the top of the 18cm (7") cake at a slight angle, positioning them on either side of the centre and 7cm (2¾") apart (AQ).

7 Glue the two larger balls of string onto the cake so they cover the posy picks. Roll two very fine sausages using a 50:50 mix of Candy Pink and White SFP. Use edible glue to fix them to the sides of the balls of string.

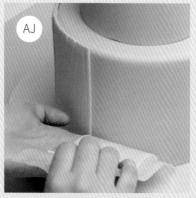

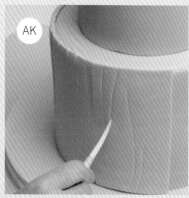

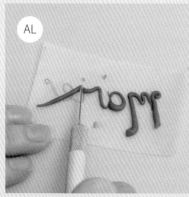

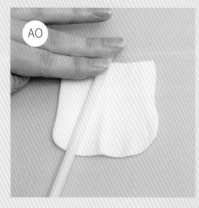

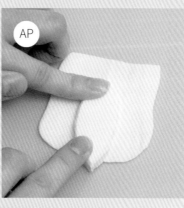

MODELS

1   Use edible glue to fix the upright cat and the sleeping cat on top of the cake.

2   Glue the mouse to the side of the cake within the semi-circular hole in the wooden panelling.

3   Glue the pouncing cat towards the right side of the front of the cake drum. Fix the smaller ball of string to the cake drum, ensuring it is within the cat's eyeline. Roll a long, thin sausage of Candy Pink SFP and glue it from the base of the ball to the cat's front paw. Trim the end of the string then attach the remainder running from the other side of the paw over the ear.

PARTY PUPPIES

These pesky pups have been causing havoc! Adapt the colours and expressions to resemble your own pets and make the design your own.

PUG

SK HD Sugar Modelling Paste: 45g (1½oz) Beige, 5g (<¼oz) Black, 10g (¼oz) Brown, 5g (<¼oz) Green, 10g (¼oz) White and 2g (<¼oz) Yellow

SK Professional Paste Food Colour: Teddy Bear Brown

BOSTON TERRIER

SK HD Sugar Modelling Paste: 30g (1oz) Black, 5g (<¼oz) Green, 50g (1¾oz) White and 2g (<¼oz) Yellow

DACHSHUND

SK HD Sugar Modelling Paste: 50g (1¾oz) Brown, 20g (¾oz) Black, 5g (<¼oz) Green, 2g (<¼oz) Pink and 25g (>¾oz) White

LABRADOR

SK HD Sugar Modelling Paste: 2g (<¼oz) Black, 5g (<¼oz) Green, 2g (<¼oz) Pink, 135g (4¾oz) White and 2g (<¼oz) Yellow

SK Professional Paste Food Colour: Teddy Bear Brown

CAMPING CAKE

SK Sugarpaste: 1.1kg (2lb 6¾oz) Iced Mint

Round cake drum: 30.5cm (12")

Round cake card: 15cm (6")

Round, filled, crumb-coated sponge cake, 12.5cm (5") deep: 15cm (6")

Template, see page 180

SK HD Sugar Modelling Paste: 40g (1½oz) Green, 100g (3½oz) White and 5g (<¼oz) Yellow

SK Professional Paste Food Colours: Poppy and Teddy Bear Brown

SK Professional Dust Food Colour: Chestnut

Piping gel: 1tbsp clear

Floral wire: 22-gauge white

Tinkertech Two Six-Petal Blossom Cutter: 1.5cm (½")

1.5cm (½") width satin ribbon: 1m (1yd 3³/₈") pale green

IMPORTANT NOTE

Ensure that the recipient of the cake is aware that it contains inedible items which must be removed before the cake is served.

PUG

1 Knead Teddy Bear Brown paste food colour into 45g (1½oz) of beige modelling paste to make a golden brown colour.

2 Roll 30g (1oz) of golden brown modelling paste into a 3.5cm (1³⁄₈") long sausage for the head. Trim away a small piece of paste from one end of the shape to create a flat base. Place your fingers on either side of the shape, just above the cut edge, and gently roll from side to side to form an indentation on each side. Gently press a large ball tool into the front of the shape to form wells for the eyes.

3 Knead a small ball of black modelling paste into 10g (¼oz) of brown modelling paste to make a darker shade of brown. Roll two small balls of the dark brown paste and press them into the wells for the eye sockets. Use your fingers and a ball tool to work the dark brown paste into the wells so their area is entirely covered. Press a smaller ball tool into the inner edge of each eye to form the eye sockets (A). Use a Dresden tool to draw curved lines around the upper and outer edges of the eye area, starting between the eyes.

4 For the muzzle, shape a marble-sized ball of dark brown modelling paste, as shown (B). Fix the paste to the face, just below the eyes. Use a Dresden tool to draw in the mouth (C). Use your fingers to push the upper lip downwards a little so it overhangs the lower lip.

5 Roll two small balls of white modelling paste and push them into the eye sockets. Use a ball tool to add a further well to the top edge of each eye and fill each with a ball of

black modelling paste (D, E). Add a tiny dot of white modelling paste to the top of each eye for a highlight.

6 Roll a very small ovoid of black modelling paste and glue it to the top of the muzzle for the nose. Use a mini ball tool to add small dots to the muzzle on either side of the nose.

7 For the ears, shape two pea-sized balls of dark brown modelling paste into thin triangles. Glue one edge of each triangle to the top of the head then bend the points down towards the face.

8 For the body, shape 12g (<½oz) of golden brown modelling paste into a ball and flatten it slightly. Shape 5g (<¼oz) of green modelling paste into a large disc and place it on top of the body. Glue a small ball of yellow modelling paste to the front of the disc. Glue the head on top of the disc.

9 Use a Dresden tool to draw wrinkles in the pug's body.

10 For the paws, roll two pea-sized balls of golden brown modelling paste. Use a Dresden tool to draw two lines on the edge of each ball for the toes. Glue the paws to the front of the body.

BOSTON TERRIER

1 Knead 25g (>¾oz) of black modelling paste into 40g (1½oz) of white modelling paste to make a dark grey colour.

2 Roll 35g (1¼oz) of dark grey modelling paste into an egg shape. Use a Dresden tool to draw three lines on the front of the body to create the front legs (F). Hold the side

of your little finger against the side of the body and gently rub it back and forth in a curve to create the haunch. Repeat on the opposite side. Use a Dresden tool to define the line between the haunches and the body (G).

3 Roll two small balls of dark grey modelling paste and use a Dresden tool to draw two lines in the front of each one to create the toes. Glue the paws under the front legs. Repeat using two slightly larger balls and glue the rear paws under the haunches.

4 Push a cocktail stick down through the neck, leaving approximately 2cm (¾") exposed at the top to support the head.

5 Roll a small piece of white modelling paste into a cone and flatten it into a teardrop. Glue the teardrop to the dog's chest.

6 Flatten a ball of green modelling paste into a disc and glue it on top of the dog's neck. Glue a small disc of yellow modelling paste just below the green disc to make the tag.

7 Roll 25g (>¾oz) of dark grey modelling paste into a ball. Roll 5g (<¼oz) of white modelling paste into a ball and pinch out a sausage shape from one side (H). Place the thinner section of the white paste over the top of the ball of dark grey paste and gently smooth the two sections together to join them (I). Pinch the larger end of the ball into a muzzle shape.

8 Roll a tiny ball of black modelling paste into an ovoid and glue it to the tip of the muzzle for the nose. Use a Dresden tool to draw a w-shaped mouth on the front of the muzzle (J).

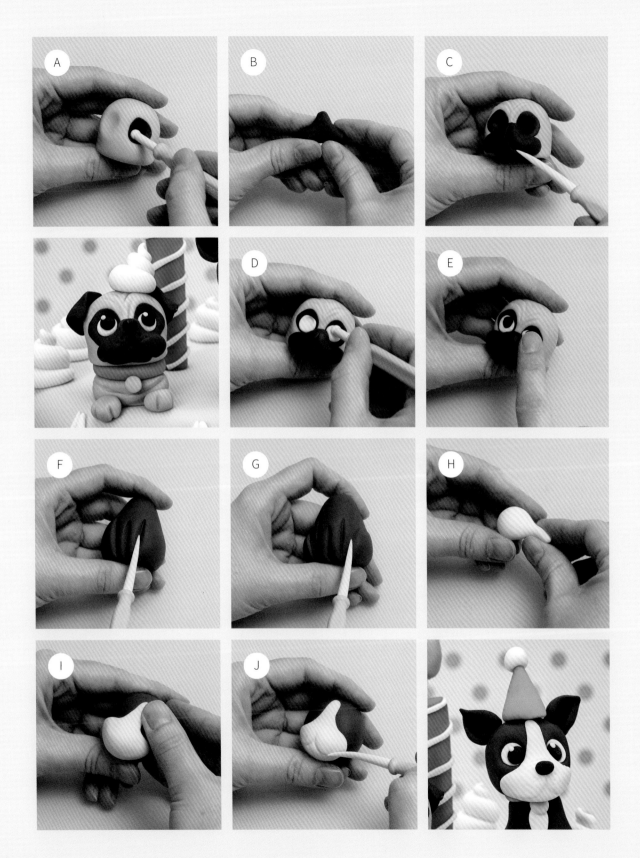

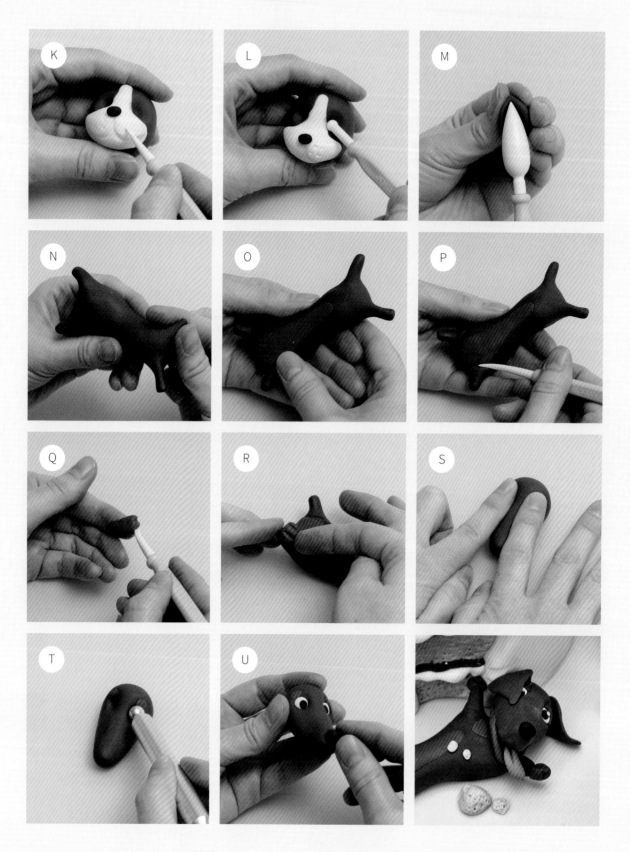

Add creases to the top of the muzzle where it joins the face. Press a mini ball tool into the cheeks to create dots for the whiskers (K).

9   Press a large ball tool into the face on either side of the white stripe then smooth away any harsh edges created by the tool. Press a smaller ball tool into the inner edge of each well to create the eye sockets (L). Fill the eye sockets with balls of white modelling paste and gently flatten them into the wells with your fingers. Press a small ball tool into the inner edge of each eye then fill each well with a small ball of black modelling paste. Add two tiny balls of white modelling paste for highlights. Use edible glue to fix the head on top of the green disc.

10   Roll a piece of dark grey paste into a cone shape. Press a rounded cone tool into the side of the cone then shape the paste around it with your fingers (M). Repeat to create a second ear then use edible glue to attach them to the dog's head.

TOP TIP

Find out how to make the Boston terrier's party hat in the Models section on page 93.

DACHSHUND

1   Knead together 30g (1oz) of brown modelling paste, 15g (½oz) of black modelling paste and 20g (¾oz) of white modelling paste to create a dark brown colour.

2   Roll 40g (1½oz) of dark brown paste into an 8cm (3¹/₈") long sausage shape and thin the centre slightly. Gently pinch and pull the paste

at one end of the sausage to create two short legs. Repeat at the opposite end to create two slightly longer legs (N).

3   Roll a piece of brown modelling paste into a pear shape then flatten it. Attach the paste to the dachshund's belly and use your fingers to blend the paste at the join (O). Repeat using a small ball of brown modelling paste for the upper chest. Use a mini ball tool to create the belly button. Use a Dresden tool to draw creases at the base of each leg (P). For the tail, roll a small ball of dark brown modelling paste into a tapered sausage and glue it in place.

4   Roll two teardrop shapes of brown modelling paste. Use a Dresden tool to draw two lines in the wide end of each teardrop to represent toes (Q). Use edible glue to attach the paws to the shorter legs (R). Repeat to add front paws to the longer legs, this time using balls of paste.

5   Flatten a ball of green modelling paste into a disc and glue it onto the dachshund's neck. Push a 5cm (2") long cocktail stick into the dog's neck, leaving approximately 1.5cm (½") exposed to support the head.

6   For the head, shape 20g (¾oz) of dark brown modelling paste into a

teardrop. Hold your index fingers over the shape, with your fingertips over the wider end, and gently press down to create the bridge of the nose (S).

7   Add a very small disc of brown modelling paste above each eye socket and blend the paste into the head using your fingers. Press a ball tool into the wells created by your fingertips to create the eye sockets (T). Fill each eye socket with a small ball of white modelling paste. Use a small ball tool to create a well in the base of each eye and fill these with black modelling paste. Add a small highlight to each eye using white modelling paste. Roll two very small balls of dark brown modelling paste into tapered sausages and gently flatten them. Glue one shape along the upper edge of each eye to form the eyelids.

8   Roll a ball of black modelling paste and use edible glue to attach it to the tip of the muzzle for the nose (U).

9   Press the broad end of a Dresden tool into the end of the muzzle to turn it upwards slightly. Use your fingers to gently pinch and shape the upper jaw. Shape a marble-sized ball of brown modelling paste to fit beneath the upper jaw, blending the paste at the join but leaving the

mouth open (V). Use a large ball tool to cup the centre of the lower jaw (W).

10 Use a Dresden tool to draw a line starting at the open mouth and running along either side of the head to continue the smile. Finish by pressing a mini ball tool into each end to create dimples. Roll a sausage of pink modelling paste and glue it just inside the open mouth. Use a Dresden tool to draw a line in the centre of the tongue.

11 Glue the head on top of the collar, pushing it down onto the cocktail stick protruding from the neck.

12 For the ears, shape 4g (<¼oz) of dark brown modelling paste into a cone then flatten it into a triangle. Use edible glue to attach one of the long edges to the top of the head, allowing the tip to fall over the face. Repeat to create a second ear.

LABRADOR

1 Knead a little Teddy Bear Brown paste food colour into 130g (4½oz) of white modelling paste to make a pale golden colour.

2 Roll 75g (2½oz) of pale golden paste into an egg shape. Use the pointed end of a Dresden tool to draw four lines on the front of the body to outline the front legs. Hold the side of your little finger against the side of the body and gently rub it back and forth in a curve to create the haunch. Repeat on the opposite side. Use a Dresden tool to define the line between the haunches and the body.

3 Roll two small balls of pale golden paste and use a Dresden tool to draw two lines in the front of each one to create the toes. Glue the paws under the front legs. Repeat using two slightly larger balls and glue the rear paws under the haunches.

4 Roll 5g (<¼oz) of pale golden paste into a long cone for the tail and glue it to the back of the body.

5 Roll 5g (<¼oz) of green modelling paste into a ball then flatten it into a disc. Use edible glue to attach the disc to the top of the Labrador's body. Attach a tiny disc of yellow modelling paste to the front of the collar using edible glue.

6 Roll 40g (1½oz) of pale golden modelling paste into a ball. Place the sides of your hands on the top edge of the ball and gently roll them to extrude the muzzle (X). Press your fingers into the paste on either side of the muzzle to shape the bridge of the nose (Y). Press the broad end of a Dresden tool into the underside of the muzzle to divide it in half (Z). Use your fingers to shape the upper lips and the top of the muzzle where it joins the face. Use a mini ball tool to make three indentations on each of the upper cheeks. Use the pointed end of a Dresden tool to draw a smile running from the upper lips towards the eyes. Make an indentation at each end of the smile using a mini ball tool (AA). Roll a small ovoid of black modelling paste and glue it to the tip of the muzzle for the nose.

7 Press a ball tool into the face on either side of the muzzle to create the eye sockets (AB). Fill the eye sockets with balls of white modelling paste and gently flatten them into the wells with your fingers. Press a small

ball tool into the lower left edge of each eye then fill each well with a small ball of black modelling paste. Add a tiny ball of white modelling paste to each eye for a highlight. Use a Dresden tool to draw a curved line above the inner corner of each eye.

8 Roll a sausage of pink modelling paste and glue it just inside the open mouth. Use a Dresden tool to draw a line in the centre of the tongue. Use edible glue to fix the head on top of the green disc.

9 For the ears, shape 4g (<¼oz) of pale golden modelling paste into a cone then flatten it into a triangle. Use edible glue to attach one of the long edges to the top of the head, allowing the tip to fall over the side of the face. Repeat to make and attach a second ear.

MAKE THE CAKE

COVERING

1 Use 500g (1lb 1¾oz) of Iced Mint sugarpaste to cover the cake drum (See page 30).

2 Trace the template (on page 180) onto a piece of greaseproof paper. Line up the base of the template with the bottom edge of the cake, cut around it and remove the cake from within the outline to a depth of 1.5cm (½"). Apply a layer of buttercream to the cut-out area. Use a pair of scissors to trim the 15cm (6") cake card to match the new shape of the cake. Spread a small amount of buttercream onto the cut 15cm (6") cake card and place the cake on top.

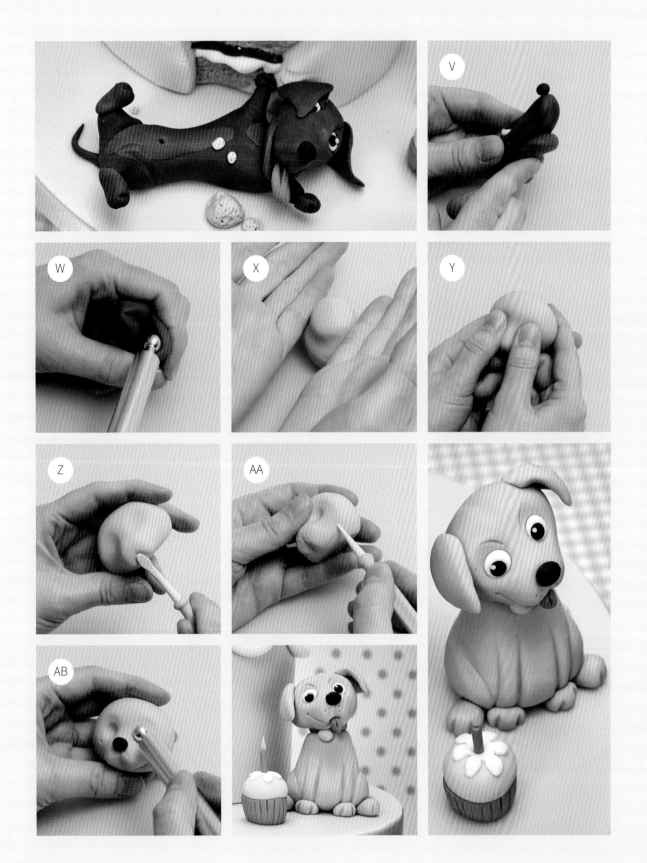

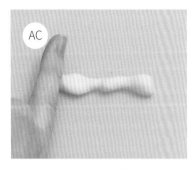

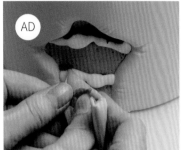

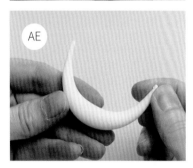

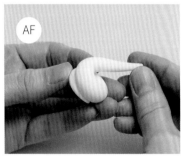

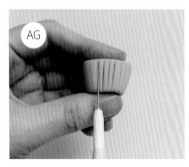

3 Use a pastry brush to apply a thin layer of cooled, boiled water to the surface of the cake. Roll out the remaining Iced Mint sugarpaste to a 4mm (³/₁₆") thickness. Lay the sugarpaste over the cake and use your hands to smooth it over the top and side. Work the sugarpaste into the cut-out area. Finish with a cake smoother. Trim away the excess sugarpaste with a sharp knife.

4 Use a Dresden tool to mark lines around the outer edge of the cut-out area.

5 Allow the cake and drum to firm for 24 hours.

DECORATING

1 Colour 30g (1oz) of white modelling paste golden brown using Teddy Bear Brown paste food colour. Roll out the golden brown paste to a 5mm (¼") thickness. Use the template to cut the paste to the size of the cut-out section then fix it inside the well using edible glue.

2 Draw two horizontal lines in the paste using the pointed end of a Dresden tool. Use a mini ball tool to add a cake-like texture to the paste. Lightly brush the golden brown paste with Chestnut dust food colour.

3 Knead a tiny amount of yellow modelling paste into a 10g (¼oz) of white modelling paste to make an off-white colour. Roll the off-white paste into two uneven sausage shapes to represent cake filling (AC). Use edible glue to fix them into the horizontal lines.

4 Colour 1tbsp of clear piping gel with Poppy paste food colour. Transfer the red piping gel to a piping bag and pipe a thin line above each of the off-white stripes to represent jam (AD).

5 Attach the cake towards the back of the cake drum using a little royal icing.

6 For the drop-line piping, divide 45g (1½oz) of white modelling paste into nine balls. Roll each ball into a 10cm (4") long sausage shape with tapered ends. Gently bend each length into a U shape (AE). Use edible glue to fix the sausages in a drop-line arrangement around the top edge of the cake.

7 For the candle, roll 20g (¾oz) of green modelling paste into a sausage shape with one end wider than the other. Trim the sausage to an 8cm (3¹/₈") length. Push a wooden barbecue skewer through the centre of the cake and trim it so that 7cm (2¾") is visible above the surface. Push the candle over the skewer and fix it in place with edible glue. Roll a small piece of white modelling paste into a very thin sausage shape and wrap it around the candle in a spiral. For the flame, roll a marble-sized ball of yellow modelling paste into a teardrop shape. Gently twist the pointed end and insert a 5cm (2") length of 22-gauge white floral wire into the wider end. Allow the flame to set. Once set, insert the wire into the top of the candle.

8 For the piped swirls, divide 35g (1¼oz) of white modelling paste into seven even balls. Roll each ball into a sausage shape, tapering one end. Starting with the wider end, curl the paste into a spiral (AF). Use edible glue to fix six of the swirls around the rear half of the top edge of the cake, spacing them evenly. Set the final swirl aside for the top of the pug's head.

9 For the cupcake, shape 15g
   (½oz) of green modelling paste
into a cone then use a sharp knife
to trim away the top and bottom.
Use a scribing tool to mark lines
around the edge of the cupcake case
(AG). Shape 5g (<¼oz) of Iced Mint
sugarpaste into a dome and glue
it on top of the cupcake case. Roll
out a little white modelling paste into
a thin sheet and cut out one flower
using the six-petal cutter. Use your
fingers to gently stretch each petal.
Glue the flower shape on top of the
dome. Roll a tiny sausage of green
modelling paste and glue it on top of
the cupcake. Finish with a tiny cone of
yellow modelling paste for the flame.
Set the cupcake aside until needed.

10 Wrap pale green ribbon
    around the edge of the cake
drum and fix it in place using double-
sided tape.

MODELS

1 Use edible glue to fix the pug
   and the Boston terrier in the
opening between the swirls on the top
of the cake. Glue the final white swirl
on top of the pug's head.

2 Knead together 2g (<¼oz) each
   of white and green modelling
paste to create a pale green colour.
Roll the pale green paste into a cone
and attach it to the top of the Boston
terrier's head, between the ears. Roll
a small ball of white modelling paste
and fix it to the point of the cone
using edible glue.

3 Glue the dachshund in front of the
   cut-out portion of the cake. Roll
some of the remaining golden brown
modelling paste into small balls of
various sizes and use a mini ball tool to
add a cake-like texture to the surface.
Glue the crumbs on and around the
dachshund.

4 Use edible glue to fix the Labrador
   towards the right side of the cake
drum. Glue the cupcake in front of
the Labrador, making sure the cake is
sitting in the dog's eye line.

SPOOKY CHARACTERS

These cute cupcakes feature Halloween favourites with a kawaii twist. There's so much flexibility with this project, simply mix and match the models or increase the sizes for larger celebration cakes.

YOU WILL NEED

PUMPKINS

SK HD Sugar Modelling Paste: 20g (¾oz) Black, 6g (¼oz) Orange, 6g (¼oz) White and 5g (<¼oz) Yellow

Round cutter: 2cm (¾")

PME Mini Scallop Tool

SK Professional Dust Food Colour: Jet Black

CAULDRON

SK HD Sugar Modelling Paste: 8g (¼oz) Black, 5g (<¼oz) Pink and 10g (¼oz) White

SK Professional Dust Food Colours: Edelweiss and Jet Black

BAT

SK HD Sugar Modelling Paste: 8g (¼oz) Black, 5g (<¼oz) Pink and 10g (¼oz) White

SK Professional Dust Food Colour: Jet Black

SKULL

SK HD Sugar Modelling Paste: 5g (<¼oz) Black, 5g (<¼oz) Pink and 12g (½oz) White

SK Professional Dust Food Colour: Edelweiss

FPC Tiny Decoration Mould

MINI GHOSTS

SK HD Sugar Modelling Paste: 5g (<¼oz) Pink and 5g (<¼oz) White

SK Professional Dust Food Colour: Jet Black

CUPCAKES

SK Sugarpaste: 60g (2oz) Zesty Orange

CMC cellulose gum

Round cutters: 2cm and 5.8cm (¾" and 2¼")

4 cupcakes, baked in black cases

50g (1¾oz) buttercream

PUMPKINS

1 Knead together 6g (<¼oz) each of orange and white modelling paste.

2 Roll 6g (<¼oz) of the pale orange modelling paste into a ball. Flatten the ball very slightly then use a Dresden tool to mark lines running from the centre point on the base to the centre point on the top, dividing it into segments (A).

3 Repeat step 2 using a pea-sized ball of pale orange modelling paste. Save a small ball of the pale orange paste before moving on to the next step.

4 Combine the remaining pale orange modelling paste with an equal quantity of yellow modelling paste. Set aside a small piece of the yellowy orange paste then divide the rest in half. Repeat step 2 using one portion of the paste.

5 Roll the second piece of yellowy orange paste into a pear shape and mark lines over the surface, as with the other pumpkins. Use a small ball tool to make a well in the top of each pumpkin.

6 Knead 5g (<¼oz) of black modelling paste into the same amount of white modelling paste. Roll out 5g (<¼oz) of the dark grey modelling paste into a thin sheet and cut out a disc using the 2cm (¾") round cutter.

7 Roll a pea-sized ball of dark grey modelling paste into a cone and flatten the base (B). Glue the cone on top of the disc, positioning it in the centre of the circle.

8 Roll out the remaining pale orange modelling paste into a thin sheet and cut out a 2mm x 4cm (¹/₁₆" x 1½") strip. Use edible glue to fix the strip around the base of the cone (C). Set the witch's hat aside to firm.

9 Roll a small piece of dark grey modelling paste into a sausage shape with tapered ends (D). Fold the sausage in half and hold the two tapered ends together. Slowly twist the two strands together to form the unicorn horn (E). Trim the widest end of the horn flat (F). Fix the horn in place in the well on top of the medium-sized round pumpkin.

10 To make the unicorn ears, roll two very small balls of dark grey modelling paste into cones. Repeat with two even smaller balls of the leftover pale orange modelling paste. Place one orange cone on top of each dark grey cone and gently press to combine and flatten the two shapes (G). Trim the wide end of each cone flat then glue them on either side of the horn for the ears.

11 Roll three tiny pieces of dark grey modelling paste into teardrops and fix them in front of the horn for the mane.

12 Roll two tiny pieces of dark grey modelling paste into cones and fix one into the well on each of the smallest two pumpkins using edible glue.

13 Mix Jet Black dust food colour with a little clear alcohol, e.g. vodka or gin, to make a paint. Use a small paintbrush to paint carved pumpkin faces on the three larger pumpkins (H). Use the PME mini scallop tool as a stamp for a curved mouth and eyes (I).

14 Use edible glue to fix the witch's hat on top of the large pumpkin.

CAULDRON

1 Knead 8g (¼oz) of black modelling paste into the same amount of white modelling paste. Roll 12g (½oz) of the dark grey paste into a ball and the rest into a 5mm (¼") diameter sausage shape. Glue the sausage around the top of the ball in a ring.

2 Mix Edelweiss dust food colour with clear alcohol, e.g. vodka or gin, to make a paint. Dip the end of a small ball tool into the white paint and use it to print two dots onto the front of the cauldron approximately 1cm (³/₈") apart (J). Dip the mini scallop tool into the paint and stamp a smile between the two dots. Use a small paintbrush to paint a curved white eyebrow above each eye. Mix up a little black paint using Jet Black paint food colour. Dip a smaller ball tool into the Jet Black paint and use it to add a pupil to each of the white dots.

3 Divide 5g (<¼oz) of pink modelling paste into 15–20 balls of various sizes. Set three of the balls aside and glue the rest inside the ring on top of the cauldron.

4 Roll two balls of white modelling paste and glue them towards the front of the pile of pink balls. Dip the end of a small ball tool into the Jet Black paint and use it to print a pupil in the centre of each white ball (K).

5 Once the cauldron is attached to your chosen cake or cupcake, fix the remaining pink balls at its base.

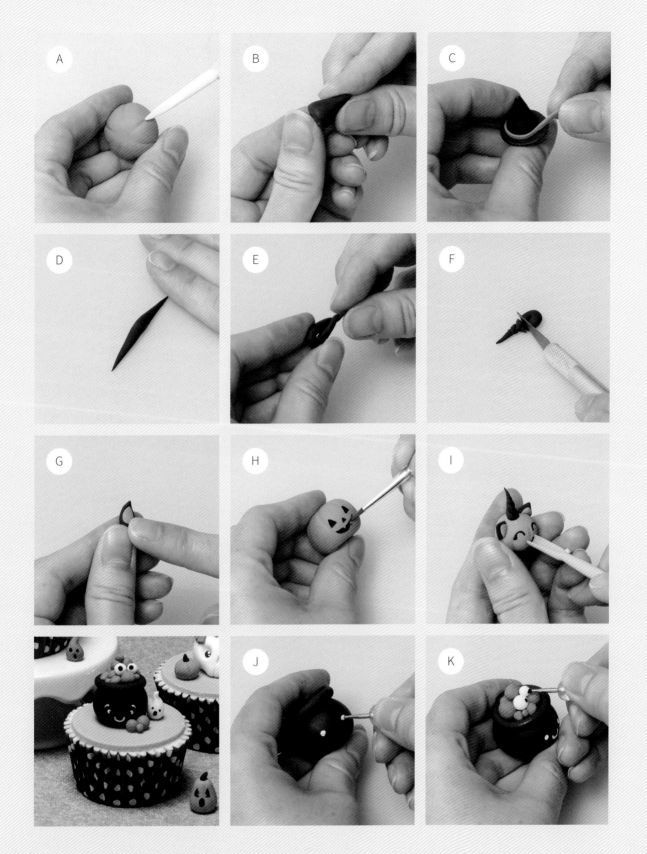

BAT

1 Knead 8g (¼oz) of black modelling paste into the same amount of white modelling paste. Roll 12g (½oz) of dark grey modelling paste into an egg shape (L). Press the wide end of a Dresden tool into the narrower end of the shape (M). Use your fingers to enhance the points on either side of the indentation.

2 Press a ball tool into the front of the shape to form two wells for the eyes. Use a mini scallop tool to make an indentation for the mouth between the eye sockets. Use a ball tool to create two capsule-shaped wells on either side of the mouth (N).

3 For the feet, slightly flatten two very small balls of dark grey modelling paste. Press a craft knife into one side of each ball twice to form three toes (O). Use edible glue to fix the feet to the base of the body.

4 Fill the eye sockets with small balls of white modelling paste. Fill the capsule-shaped wells with small sausages of pink modelling paste. Mix a little Jet Black dust food colour with clear alcohol, e.g. vodka or gin, to make a paint. Dip a mini ball tool into the black paint and add a pupil to the inner edge of each eye (P).

5 Roll a pea-sized ball of dark grey modelling paste into a teardrop shape and flatten it slightly. Place two fingers halfway up one side of the shape and gently press down (Q). Pinch the paste in the centre to a point. Use your fingers to enhance the three points. Press a Dresden tool into the paste between each point (R). Repeat to make a second wing. Use edible glue to fix the wings to either side of the body (S).

SKULL

1 Roll 12g (½oz) of white modelling paste into an egg shape and flatten the narrower end slightly. Use your fingers to shape the paste around the narrow end so that it is more pronounced.

2 Press a craft knife into the flattened base three times to mark the teeth (T). Enhance the shape of the teeth with a Dresden tool.

3 Push a ball tool into the area above the teeth to form the eye sockets (U).

4 To make the nose, press a small ball tool into the centre of the face to create two indentations approximately 2mm (¹/₁₆") apart. Press

the ball tool into the paste above the two dots and work it down to each dot to form an upside down V shape (V).

5 Glue a tiny ball of black modelling paste in the lower section of each eye socket. Dip the end of a mini ball tool in white paint and use it to print two dots on each eye, one smaller and one larger.

6 Press a small ball of pink modelling paste into the Tiny Decoration mould to create a small bow. Glue the bow on the left side of the skull.

MINI GHOSTS

1 Place a pea-sized ball of white modelling paste in the palm of your hand. Apply light pressure to one side of the ball and slowly roll to elongate it into a point. Bend the point into an S shape.

2 Mix a little Jet Black dust food colour with clear alcohol, e.g. vodka or gin, to make a paint. Dip the end of a small ball tool in black paint and use it to print two eyes and an open mouth on the white shape.

3 Repeat steps 1–2 using pink modelling paste to make a second mini ghost.

MAKE THE CUPCAKES

CUPCAKE TOPPERS

1 Knead ¼tsp of CMC into 60g (2oz) of Zesty Orange sugarpaste.

2 Roll the treated paste out to a 2–3mm (¹/₁₆") thickness. Cut out four discs using the 5.8cm (2¼") round cutter. Place the discs on a flat foam pad to firm for 12 hours.

FINISHING TOUCHES

1 Flat-ice the cupcakes using 50g (1¾oz) of buttercream (see page 32). Allow the buttercream to set at room temperature for approximately two hours.

2 Glue the witch pumpkin and unicorn pumpkin in the centre of one of the orange sugarpaste discs.

3 Glue the cauldron in the centre of another orange sugarpaste disc with the loose pink balls beside it. Glue the white mini ghost to one side of the cauldron.

4 Glue the bat in the centre of the third orange disc. Attach the pear-shaped pumpkin to the right of the bat.

5 Glue the skull in the centre of the remaining orange disc. Attach the pink ghost to right of the skull. Glue the remaining pumpkin to the left of the skull.

6 When you are ready to serve the cupcakes, place one orange disc on top of each one.

"I really love decorating cupcakes with cute figurines. It's fun to create a little set of designs that are cohesive. You could try adapting the weights of the models in this book to make matching cupcakes to go with your cakes for an extra special birthday treat."

SANTA'S LITTLE HELPERS

Impress Christmas guests with a fun festive scene. This project is great for practising expressive faces and learning how to create movement.

ELF IN A BOX

SK HD Sugar Modelling Paste: 40g (1½oz) Beige, 40g (1½oz) Black, 85g (2¾oz) Green, 25g (>¾oz) Yellow and 15g (½oz) White

Square polystyrene cake dummy, 5cm (2") deep: 7.5cm (3")

Clear piping gel

Floral wire: 20-gauge white

SK Designer Pastel Dust Food Colour: Pastel Pink

SK Sugarpaste: 70g (2½oz) Glamour Red and 40g (1½oz) Palm Green

CMC cellulose gum

SK Sugar Florist Paste (SFP): 10g (¼oz) Poinsettia

MALE ELF

SK HD Sugar Modelling Paste: 55g (2oz) Beige, 10g (¼oz) Black, 145g (5oz) Green, 30g (1oz) Orange, 5g (<¼oz) Red, 5g (<¼oz) Yellow and 30g (1oz) White

SK Professional Paste Food Colour: Marigold

CMC cellulose gum

Floral wire: 20-gauge white

PME Star Plunger Cutter: 1cm (³/₈")

SK Sugar Florist Paste (SFP): 50g (1¾oz) Poinsettia

Polystyrene cube: 2.5cm (1")

Clear piping gel

Food colour pen: orange

FEMALE ELF

SK HD Sugar Modelling Paste: 40g (1½oz) Beige, 5g (<¼oz) Black, 35g (1¼oz) Green, 5g (<¼oz) Pink, 90g (3oz) Red, and 90g (3oz) White

SK Professional Paste Food Colour: Marigold

Round cutters: 1.5cm, 8cm and 9cm (½", 3¹/₈" and 3½")

SK Designer Pastel Dust Food Colour: Pastel Pink

Food colour pen: orange

CHRISTMAS PRESENT CAKES

SK Sugarpaste: 700g (1lb 8¾oz) Antique Lace, 740g (1lb 10½oz) Glamour Red and 390g (13¾oz) Palm Green

Oblong cake drum: 30.5cm x 35.5cm (12" x 14")

2tbsp apricot jam

Square, marzipan-covered fruit cake, 6cm (2½") deep: 2 x 12.5cm (5")

Square, marzipan-covered fruit cake, 7.5cm (3") deep: 10cm (4")

Square cake cards: 10cm and 2 x 12.5cm (4" and 5")

SK Sugar Florist Paste (SFP): 30g (1oz) Poinsettia and 60g (2oz) Cream

Stitching wheel

1.5cm (½") width satin ribbon: 1.4m (55") beige

ELF IN A BOX

1 Roll out 30g (1oz) of black modelling paste into a thin sheet. Brush the top of the 7.5cm (3") square polystyrene dummy with a thin layer of clear piping gel. Lay the black paste over the top of the dummy and trim away the excess around the top edge with a sharp knife. Push a wooden barbecue skewer into the centre.

2 Roll 50g (1¾oz) of green modelling paste into an egg shape and flatten the base. Mark a line from the base to the top of the egg using a Dresden tool (A).

3 For the arms, roll 15g (½oz) of green modelling paste into a 10cm (4") long sausage shape and cut it in half. Push a ball tool into one end of each sausage to make a well. Bend each arm slightly at the elbows.

4 For the hands, split 4g (<¼oz) of beige modelling paste in half and set the second piece aside until needed. Place your thumb and forefinger on one half of the remaining ball and roll it into a sausage. Lightly pinch and stretch the ball of paste into a mitten shape (B). Cut a V-shaped notch from one side of the hand to create the thumb. Roll the thumb between your thumb and forefinger to round off the edges. Use a craft knife to cut three lines into the paste to create the fingers (C). Round the edges, as before. Bend the fingers towards the palm of the hand then bend the thumb over the fingers to make a fist (D). Trim the wrist to fit inside the well in the arm then glue the hand in place. Repeat to make and attach the second hand.

5 Divide 6g (<¼oz) of white modelling paste in half. Roll one piece into a sausage and use a small ball tool to add a fur-like texture to the surface. Glue the sausage of paste around the wrist. Repeat to complete the second arm.

6 Cut a 20-gauge white floral wire into two 9cm (3½") lengths. Bend the wires to match the shape of the arms then carefully feed them through the arms up to the wrist. Insert the wires into the elf's body and fix them in place using edible glue (E).

7 Roll 10g (¼oz) of black modelling paste into a sausage and roll it out into a thin strip. Trim the strip to 8mm x 15cm (<³/₈" x 6"). Fix the strip around the base of the body. To make the buckle, roll out 5g (<¼oz) of yellow modelling paste into a thin sheet. Cut out a 1cm (³/₈") square then cut out the centre. Glue the buckle to the front of the belt. Roll a very small sausage of yellow modelling paste and glue it to the middle of the buckle. Fit the body over the barbecue skewer and fix it in place with edible glue (F).

8 Roll a pea-sized ball of beige modelling paste into a cylinder. Feed the cylinder down over the barbecue skewer and glue it in place on top of the body to form the neck. Roll 5g (<¼oz) of white modelling paste into a sausage and use a small ball tool to add texture to its surface (G). Glue the sausage around the base of the neck to conceal the join.

9 To make the head, roll 30g (1oz) of beige modelling paste into an egg and shape the narrow end into a point (H). Use the side of your hand to lightly indent a groove just below the midline on the pointed side. Smooth out the groove with your fingers to remove any harsh lines. Push a large ball tool into the groove twice to create wells for the eyes, leaving a 5mm (¼") gap between them (I). Smooth the outer edges of the indents. Press a smaller ball tool into the inner edge of each indent and rock the tool up and down to create an oval-shaped well for the eye socket (J).

10 Roll a very small ball of beige modelling paste into a capsule shape. Glue the nose to the bottom edge of the groove. Draw a smiling mouth using the pointed end of a Dresden tool then push a mini ball tool into each end to form dimples.

11 Fill the oval-shaped wells with two small balls of white modelling paste. Press a ball tool into the inner corner of each eye then fill the indents with a small ball of black modelling paste (K). Add a very small ball of white modelling paste to the top left corner of each pupil. Roll a very thin strip of black modelling paste, cut it in half and glue one piece around the top of each eye (L).

12 For the ears, roll two pea-sized balls of beige modelling paste into cones. Press a small ball tool into each side of the head. Brush the pointed end of the cones with edible glue and insert them into the holes. Press a small ball tool into the ears and

TOP TIP

Use pieces of food-grade foam to hold the arms in place whilst they dry.

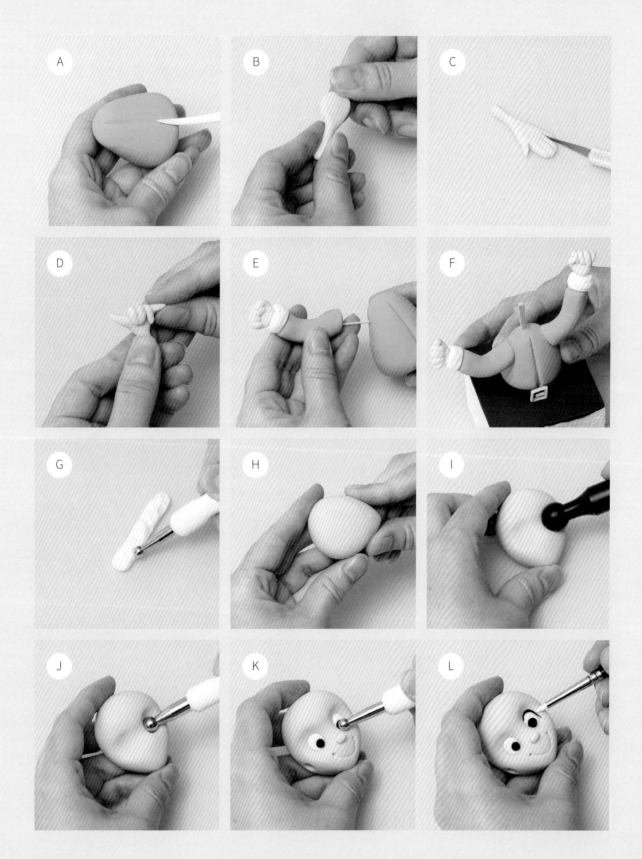

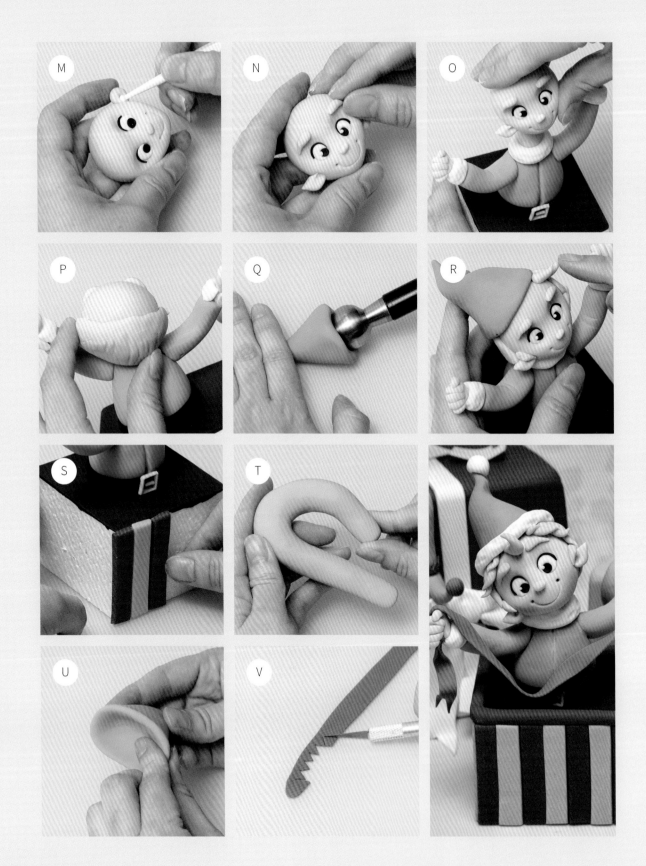

push it in towards the head to create a cupped shape (M). Use your fingers to pinch the outer ear into a point.

13 Lightly dust the cheeks with Pastel Pink dust food colour. Roll two very small pieces of yellow modelling paste into tapered sausages and glue them above the eyes (N). Use edible glue to fix the head on top of the neck at a slight angle (O). Leave the model to firm overnight.

14 Shape 15g (½oz) of yellow modelling paste to cover the back of the head, from ear to ear. Draw lines in the surface of the paste using a Dresden tool. Use edible glue to fix the shape in place (P). Roll two small cones of yellow modelling paste and glue them in front of the ears.

15 Roll 20g (¾oz) of green modelling paste into a cone. Flatten the wide end and press a large ball tool into its base to open up the centre (Q). Glue the hat on top of the head. Bend the point into an S shape.

16 Divide a small piece of yellow modelling paste into nine variously sized balls. Roll eight of the balls into long cones and glue them around the base of the hat to cover the sides of the head and the forehead (R). Roll the final ball into an elongated cone, bend the tip upwards and glue it in the centre of the forehead.

17 Roll 5g (<¼oz) of white modelling paste into a long sausage and add texture with a small ball tool. Glue the sausage around the base of the hat. Fix a ball of white modelling paste to the hat's tip.

18 Knead ¼tsp of CMC into 40g (1½oz) of Glamour Red sugarpaste and the same quantity into

40g (1½oz) of Palm Green sugarpaste. Roll the strengthened paste out to a 2mm (1/16") thickness and cut out 14 1cm x 5.5cm (3/8" x 2¼") strips of each colour. Brush clear piping gel over the sides of the cake dummy and fix the strips on top vertically, alternating the two colours (S).

19 Roll 30g (1oz) of Glamour Red sugarpaste into a 40cm (16") long sausage. Use cake smoothers to square off the edges of the sausage then use edible glue to fix it around the top edge of the box.

20 Roll 10g (¼oz) of Poinsettia SFP out into a thin sheet and cut out an 8mm x 28cm (<3/8" x 11") strip. Cut one 4.5cm (1¾") length and one 6cm (2³/8") length from the strip. Cut a V-shaped notch in one end of each of the cut pieces. Roll the straight end of each piece into a thin sausage. Brush a little edible glue on the bottom edge of each fist then attach the shorter piece to the left hand and the longer piece to the right hand. Manipulate the paste to give it shape then support it whilst it sets with some food-grade foam. Thin the ends of the remaining length and use edible glue to attach the ends to the top of each fist.

MALE ELF

1 Divide 8g (¼oz) of green modelling paste in half and roll each piece into a long cone shape for the shoes. Slightly flatten the wider ends then bend the pointed ends upwards. Roll two small balls of red modelling paste and glue them on the tips of the shoes.

2 For the legs, mix 25g (>¾oz) of green modelling paste with the

same quantity of white modelling paste then add a little Marigold paste food colour. Roll the green paste into an 18cm (7") long sausage shape, tapering both ends. Bend the shape in half then bend the right knee slightly (T). Glue the legs on top of your chosen cake. Glue a shoe to the end of each leg. Push a skewer through the legs and into the cake.

3 For the body, roll 65g (2¼oz) of green modelling paste into a cone shape. Press a large ball tool into the wider end of the cone to create a well. Use your fingers to gently pinch the paste to stretch and thin it (U). Fix the body over the legs using edible glue.

4 Knead ¼tsp of CMC into 16g (½oz) of green modelling paste. Roll the green paste into an 8cm (3¹/8") long sausage then trim one end flat. Push a ball tool into the cut end. Repeat to make a second arm. Glue the un-cut end of one arm to the left side of the body. Slightly bend a 13cm (5¼") 20-gauge white floral wire and thread it through the second arm. Push one end of the wire into the right shoulder and fix the arm in place with edible glue so it is raised. Support the arm with food-grade foam while it sets.

5 Roll out 15g (½oz) of Poinsettia SFP into a thin strip. Trim one of the long sides straight and cut a zig-zag in the other (V). Glue the trim around the cuffs of the trousers and jumper.

TOP TIP

Use SFP for fine details like ribbons and gravity defying elements as it sets really quickly and holds its shape exceptionally well.

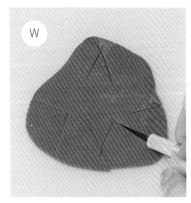

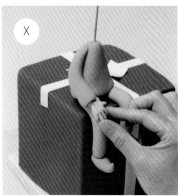

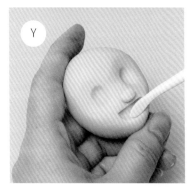

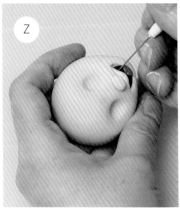

6 Roll out 10g (¼oz) of black modelling paste into a thin sheet and cut out a 5mm x 12cm (¼" x 4¾") strip. Glue the strip around the centre of the body. Roll out a small piece of yellow modelling paste and cut out a star using the plunger cutter. Glue the star in the centre of the belt.

7 Roll out 10g (¼oz) of Poinsettia SFP and cut out a 5cm (2") wide, eight-pointed star (W). Glue the star over the neck and the top of the arms. Roll a pea-sized ball of beige modelling paste into a cylinder. Feed the cylinder down over the barbecue skewer and glue it in place to form the neck. Roll a piece of Poinsettia SFP into a sausage shape and glue it around the base of the neck.

8 Repeat step 4 from the Elf in a Box instructions to make two hands using 6g (<¼oz) of beige modelling paste, this time leaving them flat rather than shaping them into fists. Glue the left hand inside the well for the wrist (X). Bend the right hand to a 90° angle at the wrist. Trim the wrist and thread it over the wire so the wire protrudes from the palm of the hand. Allow the model to firm for 48 hours.

9 Brush the 2.5cm (1") polystyrene cube with clear piping gel. Roll out 7g (¼oz) of the pale-green-coloured modelling paste into a thin sheet and lay it over the top of the cube. Smooth the paste around the top and sides then trim away the excess. Roll out 15g (½oz) of the pale-green-coloured modelling paste to a 5mm (¼") thickness. Paint edible glue over the uncovered side of the cube and place it on top of the paste. Trim the paste to fit the cube, leaving a 2mm (¹/₁₆") overhang.

10 Roll out 10g (¼oz) of Poinsettia SFP and cut out a 5mm x 24cm (¼" x 9½") strip. Cut the strip in half and glue it around the present to form crossed ribbons. Thread the present over the exposed wire on the hand and glue it in place. Cut out a 5mm x 12cm (¼" x 4¾") and 5mm x 15cm (¼" x 6") strip. Cut a V-shaped notch from one end of each strip. Glue the strips to the top of the present where the ribbons cross. Shape the loose ribbons to create movement and support until they hold their shape. Repeat step 2 from the Decoration instructions on page 113 for the present cakes to make a very small bow then attach it to the top of the present.

11 To make the head, repeat step 9 from the Elf in a Box instructions on page 104 using 45g (1½oz) of beige modelling paste. Glue a small capsule of beige modelling paste to the base of the curve for the nose. Draw in a smiling mouth using a Dresden tool then use the wider end of the tool to open it out (Y). Fill the mouth with a small piece of black modelling paste, using the Dresden tool to push it into place. Shape a very small ball of Poinsettia SFP into a semi-circle and glue it along the bottom edge of the mouth. Roll a small, tapered sausage of white modelling paste and glue it along the top edge of the mouth. Use a scribing tool to mark in individual teeth (Z).

12 Repeat steps 11–12 from the Elf in a Box instructions on page 104 to add the eyes and ears. Brush the cheeks and nose with Pastel Pink dust food colour then add freckles using an orange food colour pen. Roll two tapered sausages of orange modelling paste and glue them above the eyes for the eyebrows. Fix the head to the neck at a slight angle. Leave to firm overnight.

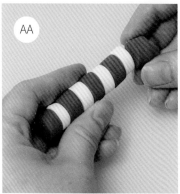

AA

13 Shape 15g (½oz) of orange modelling paste into a disc to cover the back of the head. Use a Dresden tool to mark lines in the paste. Roll 5g (<¼oz) of orange modelling paste into an elongated cone shape and flatten it until it is large enough to cover the left side of the forehead. Repeat with 6g (<¼oz) of orange modelling paste to cover the right side of the head. Use a Dresden tool to mark lines running towards the point of each piece. Glue the hair in place. Press the tip of a Dresden tool into the parting on each side to enhance the hair effect. Roll a small cone of orange modelling paste, curl the pointed end and glue it in front of the parting.

14 Roll 15g (½oz) of green modelling paste into a cone. Press a large ball tool into the base of the cone then pinch the edges with your fingers. Glue the hat on top of the elf's head and bend the point to the left.

MAKING THE FEMALE ELF

1 To create the stripy tights, roll out 35g (1¼oz) of red modelling paste to an 8mm (<³⁄₈") thickness. Cut out 10 1.5cm (½") discs. Repeat with 35g (1¼oz) of white modelling paste, this time cutting out eight discs. Glue the discs together to create two cylinders, alternating the colours (AA). Roll over the cylinders with a smoother to fix the discs together. Push a cocktail stick through each cylinder, leaving 5mm (¼") exposed at one end. Shape 10g (¼oz) of red modelling paste to join the tops of the legs and create a base for the body. Repeat step 1 from the Male Elf instructions on page 108 to make the shoes using 6g (<¼oz) of green modelling paste, omitting the red pom poms. Glue the shoes to the legs.

2 Roll out 15g (½oz) of white modelling paste and cut out an 8cm (3¹⁄₈") disc. Glue the legs on top of the disc, just off centre. Fold the other half of the disc over the top of the legs to form the underskirt. Frill the edge of the disc and glue it in place. Knead together 30g (1oz) of green modelling paste and 35g (1¼oz) of white modelling paste then add a little Marigold paste food colour. Roll out 20g (¾oz) of the pale green modelling paste into a thin sheet and cut out a 9cm (3½") disc. Repeat to add a green overskirt. Glue the legs to the top of your chosen cake, with the feet overhanging the edge.

3 For the body, shape 30g (1oz) of the pale green modelling paste into an egg and thin the waist. Press a large ball tool into the base of the shape to create a well then fit it around the top of the legs. Push a skewer through the body and into the cake.

4 For the arms, divide 12g (<½oz) of pale green modelling paste in half. Roll each piece into a 5cm (2") long tapered sausage. Push a ball tool into the wider end of the paste.

5 Repeat step 4 from the Elf in a Box instructions on page 104 to make two hands from 6g (<¼oz) of beige modelling paste, leaving them flat rather than shaping them into fists. Attach the arms to the side of the body and glue the palms to the top of the cake.

6 Roll a pea-sized ball of beige modelling paste into a cylinder and attach it to the top of the body. Roll 3g (<¼oz) of white modelling paste into a tapered sausage and use edible glue to fix it around the neck and onto the chest for the collar.

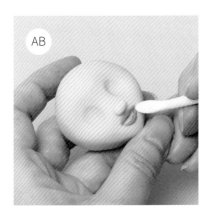

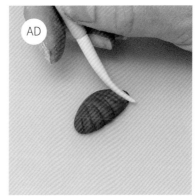

7 To make the head, repeat step 9 from the Elf in a Box instructions on page 104 using 35g (1¼oz) of beige modelling paste. Glue a small capsule of beige modelling paste to the base of the curve for the nose. Draw in a semi-circular mouth using a Dresden tool then use the wider end to open it out. Fill the mouth with white modelling paste. Press a scribing tool into either side of the mouth to increase the smile then use a mini ball tool to add dimples. Roll two very small tapered sausages of pink modelling paste and glue them along the top and bottom of the mouth, making the top lip thinner than the bottom lip (AB).

8 Repeat steps 11–12 from the Elf in a Box instructions on page 104 to add the eyes and ears. Brush the cheeks and nose with Pastel Pink dust food colour then add freckles using an orange food colour pen. Glue two tapered sausages of red modelling paste above the eyes for the eyebrows. Fix the head on top of the neck at a slight angle and leave the model to firm overnight.

9 Shape 5g (<¼oz) of red modelling paste into a thin disc to cover the back of the head. Roll 30g (1oz) of red modelling paste into 10 tapered sausage shapes. Use a Dresden tool to draw vertical lines along the length of each shape (AC). Glue eight of the sausages around the back of the head, starting at the rear and working around to the front. Glue the final two sausages in front of the ears, one on each side. Curl the ends upwards. For the fringe, shape 5g (<¼oz) of red modelling paste to fit the forehead and use a Dresden tool to draw lines over its surface (AD). Glue the fringe to the forehead.

10 Repeat step 14 from the Male Elf instructions on page 110 to make a hat using 10g (¼oz) of pale green modelling paste. Roll 3g (<¼oz) of white modelling paste into a long sausage shape and glue it around the base of the hat. Glue a small ball of white modelling paste to the tip of the hat.

MAKE THE CAKES

COVERING

1 Cover the drum using 700g (1lb 8¾oz) of Antique Lace sugarpaste (see page 30). Set the drum aside to firm for 24 hours.

2 Heat the apricot jam in a small saucepan or the microwave until it bubbles, then allow it to cool slightly. Spread a little of the jam over the surface of the 12.5cm (5") cake card and place one of the 12.5cm (5") fruit cakes on top. Fix the remaining 12.5cm (5") cake and the 10cm (4") cake on top of the corresponding cake cards in the same way.

3 Make up the royal icing according to the instructions on the packet. Spread 1tbsp of royal icing over the top of one of the 12.5cm (5") cakes then place the second 12.5cm (5") cake on top.

4 Use 700g (1lb 8¾oz) of Glamour Red sugarpaste to cover the double-height cake and 350g (12¼oz) of Palm Green sugarpaste to cover the 10cm (4") cake (see page 28). Use a Dresden tool to mark V-shaped fold lines on two opposite sides of the cake.

TOP TIP

To make your models look female, try adding a small flick of Black modelling paste to the edges of the eyes to give her eyelashes, a little more Pink dust to the cheeks for a rosy glow and pale Pink or Red tapered sausages to the mouth to give her a lipsticked pout.

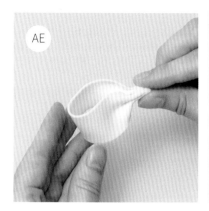

5 Roll out 350g (12¼oz) of Palm Green sugarpaste to a 4mm (³/₁₆") thickness. Repeat step 4 to cover the 10cm (4") cake. Set the cakes aside to firm for 24 hours.

DECORATION

1 Roll 30g (1oz) of Cream SFP into a long sausage shape. Roll the sausage out to a 1mm (<¹/₁₆") thickness and cut out a 1.5cm x 40cm (½" x 16") strip. Glue the strip over the top and two sides of the 12.5cm (5") cake. Cut out two 1.5cm x 25cm (½" x 10") strips and glue one to each of the remaining sides of the cake, joining up with the first strip at the front and back.

2 To make a bow, roll out 20g (¾oz) of Cream SFP to a 1mm (<¹/₁₆") thickness and cut out two 2.5cm x 10cm (1" x 4") rectangles. Cut out a triangle from one end of each rectangle and pleat the un-cut ends. Glue the pleated end of each rectangle to the front of the cake where the ribbons intersect. Cut out a 2cm x 5cm (¾" x 2") rectangle and pleat the entire length. Glue one end of this rectangle on top of the join between the previous two pieces. Cut out two 2.5cm x 11cm (1" x 4 ½") rectangles. Pleat each end, as before, then bend the rectangle in half so that the two pleated ends meet (AE). Repeat for both rectangles. Glue the loops in place on either side of the bow then wrap the 2cm x 5cm (¾" x 2") rectangle around the join.

3 Roll out 15g (½oz) of Poinsettia SFP to a 1mm (<¹/₁₆") thickness and cut out a 1.5cm x 10cm (½" x 4") strip. Use the stitching wheel to add a stitch pattern down each side of the strip. Glue the strip over the top and sides of the 10cm (4") cake. Repeat to add a second strip, forming a cross over the cake.

4 Use a little royal icing to fix the red cake to the back left side of the covered cake drum and the green cake to the back right side, angling them both inwards slightly.

MODELS

1 Build the male elf and female elf figures on top of the 12.5cm and 10cm (5" and 4") cakes, as indicated in the instructions.

2 Use a little royal icing to fix the elf in a box to the front of the drum.

FINISHING TOUCHES

4 Roll out 10g (¼oz) of Cream SFP into a thin sheet and cut out three 2cm x 3cm (¾" x 1¹/₈") rectangles. Use a Dresden tool to draw V shapes on two of the rectangles to make envelopes. Glue a tiny square of Poinsettia SFP in the top right corner of the third envelope for a stamp. Glue the envelopes on top of the 12.5cm (5") cake.

2 Fix beige ribbon around the edge of the cake drum using non-toxic glue, being careful not to come into contact with the sugarpaste.

PESKY MICE

Say cheese! These fun little rodants are great for topping cupcakes and larger cakes, depending on the occasion.

COLLAPSED MOUSE

SK HD Sugar Modelling Paste: 5g (<¼oz) Black and 40g (1½oz) White

SK Quality Food Colour (QFC) Paste: Pink

DIGGING MOUSE

SK HD Sugar Modelling Paste: 8g (¼oz) Black and 25g (>¾oz) White

SK Quality Food Colour (QFC) Paste: Pink

MUNCHING MOUSE

SK HD Sugar Modelling Paste: 5g (<¼oz) Black and 60g (2oz) White

SK Professional Paste Food Colours: Teddy Bear Brown

SK Quality Food Colour (QFC) Paste: Pink

Round cutter: 5mm (¼")

BABY MOUSE

SK HD Sugar Modelling Paste: 5g (<¼oz) Black and 40g (1½oz) White

SK Professional Paste Food Colours: Teddy Bear Brown and Thrift

CHEESE CUPCAKES

Round pastry cutter: 6.8cm (2⅝")

SK HD Sugar Modelling Paste: 200g (7oz) Yellow

SK Professional Dust Food Colour: Sunflower

SK Quality Food Colour (QFC) Dust: Orange

4 cupcakes baked in yellow Cases

100g (3½oz) buttercream

COLLAPSED MOUSE

1   Knead a small ball of black modelling paste into 28g (1oz) of white modelling paste to create a light grey colour.

2   Roll 15g (½oz) of light grey modelling paste into an egg shape. To create the stomach and chest, lay the egg on its side and gently press the side of your hand into the paste just above the halfway point, rocking it back and forth. Smooth out the edges of the indentation mark to narrow the chest, leaving a rounded stomach.

3   Use your finger and thumb to pinch out the paste at the base of the shape to extrude one short leg from each side. Move your fingers around the emerging leg as you pinch to avoid creating folds and creases.

4   Repeat step 3 to create an arm on the left side of the upper body (A). The right arm needs to be a little longer so, once you have extruded the paste, roll it between your fingers to lengthen it slightly.

5   Roll a small-pea-sized ball of light grey modelling paste into a 1cm (³/₈") long sausage shape. Use edible glue to attach the right arm to the body, running from the right shoulder up and over the chest. Press a mini ball tool into the centre of the stomach to create a belly button.

6   Colour 8g (¼oz) of white modelling paste pale pink using Pink paste colour. Roll a very small ball of pale pink paste into a cone shape. Place the cone on your finger, with the wider end at your fingertip. Press a scribing tool into the wide end of the shape twice to create three fingers (B).

Repeat to create a second hand. Glue the hands onto the front legs.

7   Repeat step 6 to make the feet using two slightly larger balls of pale pink paste. Use edible glue to attach one foot to the end of each leg (C).

8   Roll a marble-sized ball of pale pink modelling paste into a tapered sausage 5cm (2") long and bend it into an S-shaped curve. Pinch the wider end to flatten it a little (D). Glue the tail to the back of the body.

9   Shape 10g (¼oz) of light grey modelling paste into a cone. Thin the pointed end further and bend the tip back slightly to create the shape of the head (E). Use a scribing tool to draw three lines for the mouth in the front of the bent section (F). Press the broad end of a Dresden tool into the right side of the mouth to open it out (G). Push a mini ball tool into the edges of the smile to create dimples.

10   Lightly press your fingers into the face on either side of the nose (H). Smooth away any harsh lines around the wells using your finger. Press a medium ball tool into each of the wells to create the eye sockets (I). Press a small ball tool into the top of the head to create holes for the ears (J).

11   Fill each eye socket with a small ball of white modelling paste. Press a small ball tool into the inner edge of each eye and fill the wells with black modelling paste (K). Add a very small ball of white modelling paste to the upper left side of each pupil to create highlights. Roll a small ball of light grey modelling paste into the shape of a grain of rice and glue it over the upper edge of one eye, using a Dresden tool to guide it into position. Repeat to add an eyelid to the other eye. Glue a small tapered sausage of black modelling paste along the bottom edge of each eye lid.

12   Roll a small piece of pale pink modelling paste into an ovoid and glue it onto the tip of the nose. Repeat to create a second pale pink ovoid and glue it inside the mouth for the tongue (L). Use a scribing tool to draw a line along the centre of the tongue.

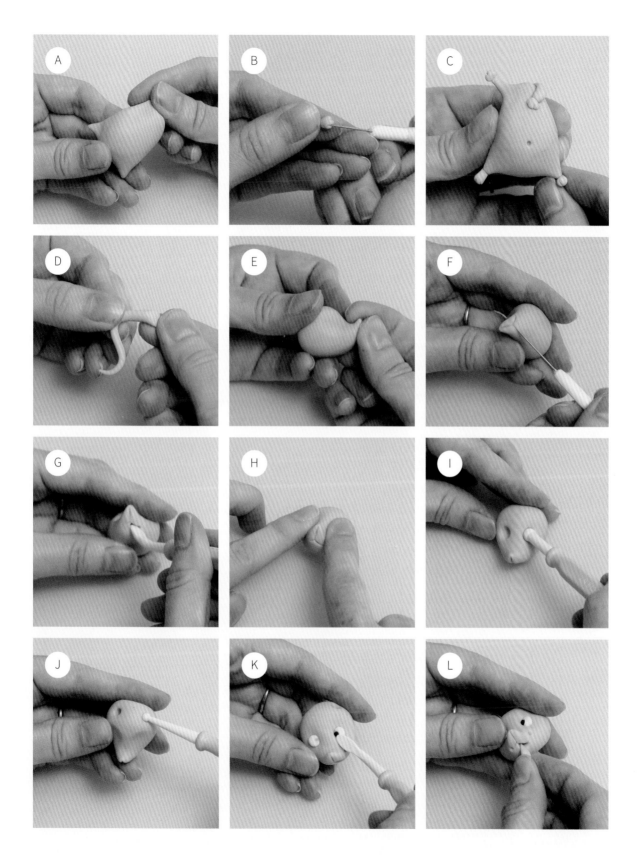

13 To make the ears, flatten a large-pea-sized ball of light grey modelling paste into a chunky disc. Roll a piece of pale pink modelling paste into ball a third of the size of the light grey ball and place it in the centre of the disc. Press a large ball tool down into the centre of the pink ball to fix the two colours together and create a cupped shape (M). Run the broad end of a Dresden tool from the centre of the cup out to one edge (N). Pinch the paste on either side of the indentation to a point (O). Repeat to make a second ear then use edible glue to fix the points into the indentations in the top of the head (P).

14 Glue the head to the mouse's body then set the mouse aside to firm overnight.

DIGGING MOUSE

1 Knead 5g (<¼oz) of black modelling paste into 10g (¼oz) of white modelling paste to create a dark grey paste and roll it into a ball.

2 Knead a tiny piece of black modelling paste into a pea-sized ball of white modelling paste to create

a pale grey paste. Shape the pale grey paste into an egg and flatten it. Place the pale grey egg shape on top of the dark grey ball and smooth the edges to create a seamless join (Q). Flatten the base of the ball to create a dome.

3 Repeat step 3 from the Collapsed Mouse instructions to extrude two 5mm (¼") long legs from the top of the dome (R).

4 Push a mini ball tool into the centre of the stomach to create the belly button.

5 Knead a little Pink paste food colour into 10g (¼oz) of white modelling paste to make a pale pink colour. Repeat step 7 from the Collapsed Mouse instructions to make and attach a foot for each leg.

6 Press a medium ball tool into the body just behind the legs. Repeat step 8 from the Collapsed Mouse instructions to make and attach a tail using pale pink modelling paste, curling the tip into a spiral (S). Set the tail aside to firm for one hour before fixing it inside the indentation at the back of the mouse using edible glue.

MUNCHING MOUSE

1 Colour 45g (1½oz) of white modelling paste warm brown using Teddy Bear Brown paste food colour. Roll 18g (⅝oz) of warm brown modelling paste into a ball then flatten the base to create a dome.

2 Press the sides of your little finger into opposite sides of the dome, creating indentations on each side for the haunches (T). Use your fingertips to further define the haunches then draw

a crease line in each side using the pointed end of a Dresden tool.

3 Knead a little Pink paste food colour into 10g (¼oz) of white modelling paste to make a pale pink colour. Repeat step 7 from the Collapsed Mouse instructions to make two feet then attach them to the underside of the body.

4 Roll a pea-sized ball of warm brown modelling paste into a 1.5cm (½") long sausage, tapered at one end. Flatten the sausage slightly and bend it into a crescent shape. Glue the arm to the body with the wider end at the shoulder and the thin end sitting on the chest (U). Repeat to make and attach a second arm.

5 Shape a small ball of yellow modelling paste into a block. Press a mini ball tool into the surface of the block to create a cheese-like texture. Glue the block of cheese to the centre of the chest. Repeat step 6 from the Collapsed Mouse instructions to make two hands then attach them between the ends of the arms and the cheese.

6 Roll a marble-sized ball of pale pink modelling paste into a tapered sausage 5cm (2") long. Glue the tail to the mouse's back, starting at the base and curling around the side of the body.

7 Roll 20g (¾oz) of warm brown modelling paste into a cone. Bend the tip of the cone upwards slightly. Pinch the top of the head between your finger and thumb to narrow it slightly (V).

8 Use a scribing tool to draw a 1cm (³⁄₈") long line down the front of the face then use the pointed end of a Dresden tool to draw a curved line at the base of the 1cm (³⁄₈") line. Press the broad end of a Dresden tool into the bottom edge of the curve to create a small indentation (W). Press a mini ball tool into each end of the curved line to create dimples.

TOP TIP

If you are not confident at drawing a curved line, try pressing the base of a round cutter or piping tip into the paste to create the shape.

9 Lightly press your fingertips into the paste halfway up the face to create two shallow wells (X). Press a medium ball tool into the wells, 8mm (¼") apart, to create the eye sockets. Press a small ball tool into the top of the head twice to create holes for the ears.

10 Repeat step 13 from the Collapsed Mouse instructions to make two ears using warm brown and pale pink modelling paste. Cut out a semi-circle from the left ear using a 5mm (¼") round cutter. Glue the ears into the holes on top of the head (Y).

11 Roll two very fine tapered sausages of warm brown modelling paste and glue one in front of each ear, forming tufts of fur. Repeat to attach a larger tuft of fur to the top of the head. Use a scribing tool to draw lines down the cone to give the impression of strands of fur.

12 Fill each eye socket with a small ball of white modelling paste. Press a small ball tool into the inner edge of each eye and fill the wells with black modelling paste. Add a very small ball of white modelling paste to the upper left side of each pupil to create highlights. Glue a small tapered sausage of black modelling paste around the top and outer edge of each eye.

13 Shape a small ball of white modelling paste into an oblong and draw a line down the centre using a scribing tool. Glue the top edge of the teeth inside the indentation at the base of the smile.

14 Roll a small piece of pale pink modelling paste into a cone and attach it to the tip of the nose. Glue the head on top of the body.

TOP TIP

If you struggle to add the white highlight to the eye, use a very small ball tool to create a shallow well where you would like the highlight to sit and then pop the White modelling paste into it. It saves chasing it around the eye trying to get it to stay in place.

BABY MOUSE

1 Colour 30g (1oz) of white modelling paste pale purple using Thrift paste food colour.

2 Roll 10g (¼oz) of pale purple modelling paste into an egg. Press a mini ball tool into the front of the egg to create the belly button.

3 Colour a marble-sized ball of white modelling paste beige using Teddy Bear Brown paste food colour. Repeat step 7 from the Collapsed Mouse instructions to make two beige feet then glue them to the base of the body.

4 Roll a pea-sized ball of pale purple modelling paste into a 3cm (1¹⁄₈") long sausage shape and cut it in half. Bend each piece to a right angle halfway along its length (Z). Glue one arm to each side of the body, wresting the wrists on the chest. Repeat step 6 from the Collapsed Mouse instructions to make two beige hands and attach them to the ends of the arms (AA).

5 Roll a piece of beige modelling paste into a tapered sausage shape 4cm (1½") long. Glue the tail to the mouse's back, bending the tip round to one side.

6 Roll 12g (½oz) of pale purple modelling paste into a cone shape. Bend the tip of the cone upwards. Use a scribing tool to draw a vertical line in the front of the face then add a curved line underneath to make the mouth. Press a Dresden tool into the paste beneath the smile to create a small well. Press a mini ball tool into each end of the smile to

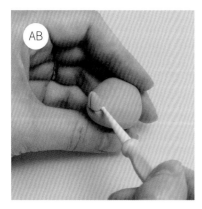

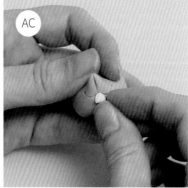

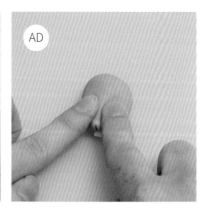

make dimples (AB). Shape a tiny piece of white modelling paste into an oblong and glue it inside the well to form the teeth (AC).

7 Lightly press your fingertips into the paste on either side of the nose, as close to the mouth as possible, to create wells for the eyes (AD). Smooth away any harsh lines with your fingers. Press a medium ball tool into the wells to create eye sockets, moving the tool slightly to increase the size of each well (AE). Fill each eye socket with a ball of white modelling paste. Press a small ball tool into the inner corner at the bottom of each eye, moving the tool to increase the size of

each well slightly. Fill each well with black modelling paste. Add a small ball of white modelling paste to each eye to form a highlight. Roll two tiny pieces of wlack modelling paste into thin tapered sausages and glue them around the top and outer edge of each eye (AF).

8 Press a small ball tool into the sides of the head. Flatten a large-pea-sized ball of pale purple modelling paste into a chunky disc. Press a large ball tool into the centre of the disc and work it over the surface of the paste to create a large well in the centre. Run the broad end of a Dresden tool over one edge of the ear then pinch the paste on either side of the thinner section to a point. Repeat to make a second ear. Glue the pointed ends the ears into

the holes created on the side of the head. Use food-safe foam to support the ears in position until they can hold their own weight.

9 Roll a tiny piece of pale purple modelling paste into a tapered sausage shape. Glue the tuft of hair on top of the baby mouse's head and curl the tip over.

10 Glue the baby mouse's head on top of its body.

TOP TIP

To create a childlike character, the eyes should be larger than an adult and closer to the mouth, leaving a larger forehead area.

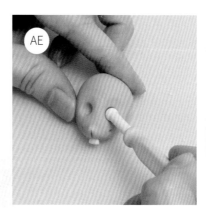

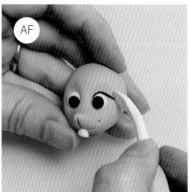

MAKE THE CUPCAKES

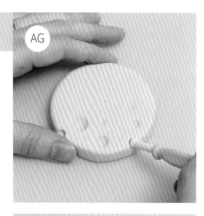

AG

CHEESE TOPPERS

1   Roll out 200g (7oz) of yellow modelling paste to a 1cm (³/₈") thickness. Cut out four discs using a 6.8cm (2⁵/₈") pastry cutter. Gently run your fingers over the top and bottom edges of the discs to round them off.

2   Press small and large ball tools into the top and sides of each disc to create indentations of various sizes and depths (AG).

3   Brush Sunflower dust food colour inside the wells then add touches of Orange dust food colour in the deeper indentations (AH). Set the cheese toppers aside to firm overnight.

CHEESE CRUMBS

1   Roll small pieces of yellow modelling paste into irregular balls.

2   Press a mini ball tool into the surface of the paste to create a cheese-like texture.

CUPCAKES

1   Flat-ice the tops of the cupcakes with buttercream using a cranked palette knife following the instructions on page 32.

2   Place one cheese topper on top of each cupcake.

MODELS

1   Use edible glue to attach one mouse to the top of each cheese topper.

2   Scatter cheese crumbs on top of and around the mice, fixing them in place with edible glue.

AH

BUNCH OF BUNNIES

Celebrate springtime with a colony or 'fluffle' of playful bunnies in flowerpots. Mix and match their poses with the suggested decorations to create your own combinations.

BUNNY EARS

SK HD Sugar Modelling Paste: 14g (½oz) Beige

SK Professional Paste Food Colour: Teddy Bear Brown

BUNNY BOTTOM

SK HD Sugar Modelling Paste: 50g (1¾oz) Beige and 5g (<¼oz) White

SK Professional Paste Food Colour: Teddy Bear Brown

PEEKING BUNNY

SK HD Sugar Modelling Paste: 70g (2½oz) Beige, 2g (<⅛oz) Black, 2g (<⅛oz) Brown and 10g (¼oz) White

SK Professional Paste Food Colour: Teddy Bear Brown

SLEEPING BUNNY

SK HD Sugar Modelling Paste: 75g (2½oz) Beige, 2g (<⅛oz) Brown and 10g (¼oz) White

SK Professional Paste Food Colour: Teddy Bear Brown

DOZY BUNNY

SK HD Sugar Modelling Paste: 110g (3¾oz) Beige, 2g (<⅛oz) Brown and 10g (¼oz) White

SK Professional Paste Food Colour: Teddy Bear Brown

FLOWERPOT CAKES

Round, filled sponge cakes, 5.5cm (2¼") deep: 5 x 7.5cm (3")

150g (5¼oz) buttercream

SK Sugarpaste: 95g (3¼oz) Bridal White, 95g (3¼oz) Coco Brown and 450g (1lb) Zesty Orange

SK Designer Paste Food Colour: Terracotta

CMC Cellulose Gum

FMM Ribbon Cutter

Piping gel: clear

SK HD Sugar Modelling Paste: 5g (<¼oz) Beige, 5g (<¼oz) Black, 45g (1½oz) Green, 25g (>¾oz) Pink, 20g (¾oz) Orange, 5g (<¼oz) Red, 5g (<¼oz) Turquoise, 100g (3½oz) White and 20g (¾oz) Yellow

BUNNY EARS

1 Knead a little Teddy Bear Brown paste food colour into 14g (½oz) of beige modelling paste to make a golden brown colour.

2 Divide the golden-brown-coloured modelling paste in half and roll each piece into a long, thin cone shape. Dust the side of your little finger with a little cornflour and gently press it into the middle of one cone to form a groove (A). Place another finger on the outer edge of the cone and begin to thin the edges. Pinch the base of the cone together to form the ear (B). Repeat to shape the second ear.

3 Bend the top of one ear over a little (C). Glue the ears together at the base then fix them on top of your chosen cake.

BUNNY BOTTOM

1 Knead a little Teddy Bear Brown paste food colour into 50g (1¾oz) of beige modelling paste to make a golden brown colour.

2 Roll 40g (1½oz) of golden-brown-coloured modelling paste into a ball then flatten one side to create a dome (D).

3 Roll 5g (<¼oz) of white modelling paste into a ball and glue it centrally on the top of the dome. Use a small ball tool to make indents all over the surface of the white ball to create a fluffy texture (E).

4 To make the feet, roll 4g (<¼oz) of golden-brown-coloured modelling paste into a cone and gently flatten it between your fingers. Place one finger widthways across the wider end of the cone and use another finger to gently press the wide end in towards your finger to thicken that section of paste. Press a Dresden tool into the wider end of the foot twice to mark the toes (F). Use a craft knife to cut through the indents to form individual toes (G). Use a medium ball tool to mark in the sole then a small ball tool to mark in the pads underneath the toes (H). Repeat to make a second foot. Use edible glue to fix the feet behind the dome.

PEEKING BUNNY

1 Knead a little Teddy Bear Brown paste food colour into 70g (2½oz) of beige modelling paste, aiming for a slightly different shade from the previous bunnies.

2 Divide 6g (<¼oz) of the golden-brown-coloured modelling paste in half. Roll each piece into a cone then gently flatten them. Press a Dresden tool into the fore-foot twice then use a craft knife to cut through the indents to form individual toes. Glue the paws to the front of your chosen cake, with the toes overhanging the edge.

3 Shape 15g (½oz) of the golden-brown-coloured modelling paste into a squat dome for the body and use edible glue to fix it behind the paws. Roll 5g (<¼oz) of white modelling paste into a ball for the tail and add texture using a small ball tool. Glue the tail on top of the dome.

4 For the head, roll 35g (1¼oz) of the golden-brown-coloured modelling paste into an ovoid. Press your thumbs (or a large ball tool) into the paste on either side of the centre (I). Use your fingers to smooth the outer edges of the indents. For the muzzle, roll a pea-sized ball of white modelling paste into a capsule shape. Use the pointed end of a Dresden tool to draw a line across the middle of the shape (J). Glue the muzzle in place on the face. Shape a small piece of brown modelling paste into a triangle and glue it on top of the muzzle to form the nose.

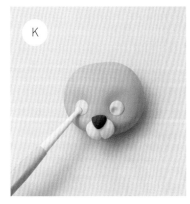

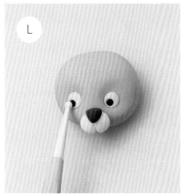

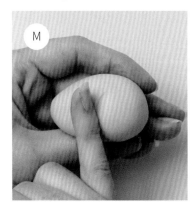

5   Press a medium-sized ball tool into the wells on either side of the muzzle to create eye sockets. Fill each indentation with a small ball of white modelling paste. Press a smaller ball tool into the inner corner of each eye then fill the indentations with a small ball of black modelling paste (K, L). Glue the head on top of the dome.

6   Repeat step 2 from the Bunny Ears instructions to make two ears. Glue the ears on top of the head and bend the left ear over the face.

SLEEPING BUNNY

1   Knead a little Teddy Bear Brown paste food colour into 75g (2½oz) of beige modelling paste to make a golden brown colour.

2   For the body, roll 35g (1¼oz) of golden-brown-coloured modelling paste into an egg. Place the side of your little finger against the wider end of the egg and gently press down to create the haunch of the left leg (M). Smooth away the indent towards the narrower end of the egg. Use a Dresden tool to draw a crease line along the indentation.

3   Repeat step 2 from the Peeking Bunny instructions to make three paws using 3g (<¼oz) of paste each. Glue one paw underneath the haunch and the other two at the front of the body.

4   Roll 5g (<¼oz) of white modelling paste into a ball and add texture using a small ball tool. Glue the tail to the back of the bunny (N).

5   Repeat steps 4–5 from the Peeking Bunny instructions to

create a head using 25g (>¾oz) of modelling paste, this time filling the eye sockets with golden-brown-coloured modelling paste, rather than white, to create closed eyes. Use a scribing tool to draw a line across the centre of each eye and add two creases on the outer edges.

6   For the ears, roll two 3g (<¼oz) balls of golden-brown-coloured modelling paste into elongated cone shapes. Gently pinch and flatten each cone between your fingers. Glue the ears to the top of the head.

DOZY BUNNY

1   Knead a little Teddy Bear Brown paste food colour into 110g (3¾oz) of beige modelling paste to make a golden brown colour. Roll 45g (1½oz) of golden-brown-coloured modelling paste into a pear shape. From the wider end, gently pinch and shape the paste on either side to draw out two short legs. Glue the body over the edge of your chosen cake, with the majority hanging over the side.

2   Create two rear paws following step 2 from the Peeking Bunny instructions. Glue one paw to the base of each leg, with the toes resting on the side of the cake. Use the same method to create two front paws, each using 4g (<¼oz) of golden-brown-coloured modelling paste. Glue the front paws on the front of the body.

3   Roll 5g (<¼oz) of white modelling paste into a ball and add texture using a small ball tool. Glue the tail in place.

4   Repeat steps 4–5 from the Peeking Bunny instructions to

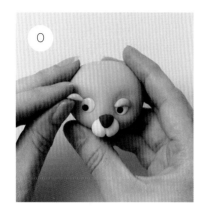

create a head using 35g (1¼oz) of modelling paste. Roll two very small pieces of golden-brown-coloured modelling paste into tapered sausage shapes and glue one over the top of each eye (O). Use your fingers to gently flatten the paste so it covers the top half of the eyeball. Glue the head to the neck, using a cocktail stick as support until it is fully adhered.

5   Repeat step 2 from the Bunny Ears instructions to make two ears using 14g (½oz) of golden-brown-coloured modelling paste. Glue the ears on top of the head.

MAKE THE CAKES

FLOWERPOT CAKES

1   Cut out a 6cm (2³/₈") disc of baking paper to use as a template. Place the template in the centre of the first 7.5cm (3") cake. With a serrated knife, trim away the sides of cake at an angle to create a flowerpot shape, using the template as a guide. Repeat to carve all the mini cakes.

2   Apply a crumb coat of buttercream to the side of each cake (see page 27). Refrigerate the cakes for approximately one hour.

3   Knead Terracotta paste food colour into 450g (1lb) of Zesty Orange sugarpaste. Roll out the terracotta-coloured sugarpaste to a 2mm (¹/₁₆") thickness. Use a pastry brush to apply a thin layer of cooled, boiled water over the surface of the cake. Lay the sugarpaste over the cake and use your hands to smooth the surface, then finish with a cake smoother. Trim away the excess sugarpaste with a sharp knife.

4   Use a Dresden tool to draw cracks and fracture lines in the sides of the pot. Repeat to cover all five cakes then set them aside to firm for at least 24 hours.

TOP TIP

Use a sharp knife to cut out a cone from the centre of each mini cake. Fill the well with orange buttercream to create a carrot-shaped surprise.

5   Once firm, carefully turn the cakes over so they sit on the narrower end. Spread a layer of buttercream over the top of each cake.

6   Knead 95g (3¼oz) of Bridal White sugarpaste into 95g (3¼oz) of Coco Brown sugarpaste. Use your hands to shape 35g (1¼oz) of the light brown sugarpaste into a 7.5cm (3") diameter mound. Use the sides of your hands and fingers to create an uneven surface with peaks and grooves (P). Glue the mound on top of one of the flowerpots. Repeat to add a soil topper to each pot.

7   Knead ¼tsp of CMC into the remaining terracotta-coloured sugarpaste. Wrap the paste well with cling film and set it aside for 30 minutes.

8   Roll out the terracotta-coloured paste to a 1–2mm (¹/₁₆") thickness. Set the ribbon cutter to a 2cm (¾") width and cut out a 26.5cm (10¼") long strip. Paint a thin layer of piping gel around the top edge of one flowerpot. Wrap the strip of paste around the top edge (Q). Use a cake smoother to smooth the paste into place. Repeat to add a rim to each flowerpot then set them aside to firm.

DECORATIONS

1   Make up a 50:50 mixture of white and green modelling paste. Roll three small pieces of pale green modelling paste into long, thin cone shapes. Use edible glue to fix the cones together into tufts of grass. Repeat to make as many tufts as you need.

2   Roll 4g (<¼oz) of pale green modelling paste into a teardrop. Flatten the shape with your fingers then use a Dresden tool to mark veins in the surface (R). Repeat to make as many leaves as you need.

3   Make up a 50:50 mixture of white and pink modelling paste. Divide 12g (<½) of the pale pink modelling paste into fifths. Roll each piece into a cone then gently flatten them with your fingers. Use edible glue to fix the petals into a flower shape. Use a Dresden tool to mark a crease along the centre of each petal (S). Make up a 50:50 mixture of white and yellow modelling paste. Roll a small piece of pale yellow modelling paste into a ball and glue it in the centre of the flower. Repeat this step using a 50:50 mixture of white and orange modelling paste to make orange flowers.

4   To make a snail, shape a large-pea-sized ball of beige modelling paste into a sausage with one tapered end. Bend the sausage to a 90° angle one third of the way in from the wider end (T). Make up a 50:50 mixture of small amounts of turquoise and pink modelling paste. Roll the mixed paste into a second sausage with one tapered end. Starting at the pointed end, roll the sausage up into a spiral (U). Glue the spiral on top of the beige paste to create a snail (V).

5   To make a ladybird, make up a 50:50 mixture of white and red modelling paste. Roll the light red modelling paste into a capsule shape and cut away one third of its length, discarding the smaller piece. Use a scribing tool to draw a line down the centre of the remaining piece of paste (W). Make up a 50:50 mixture of white and black modelling paste. Roll the paste into a capsule shape and cut away two thirds of its length. Glue the remaining third to the pale red body (X). Roll five very small balls of mixed black modelling paste and glue them on the red section of the body.

6   Glue the decorations to the tops and sides of the flowerpots, fitting them around the shape and position of each bunny.

WOODLAND CRITTERS

These adorable forest animals are having a great time on their camping trip! The playful, illustrative style makes it a great project for beginners.

YOU WILL NEED

BADGER

SK HD Sugar Modelling Paste: 15g (½oz) Black, 5g (<¼oz) Rosy Pink, 40g (1½oz) White

SK Sugar Modelling Paste:

SK Quality Food Colour (QFC) Dusts: Pink

SK Edible Paint by Natasha Collins: Jasmine

FOX

SK HD Sugar Modelling Paste: 5g (<¼oz) Black, 5g (<¼oz) Brown, 60g (2oz) Orange and 10g (¼oz) White

SK Quality Food Colour (QFC) Dusts: Pink

SK Edible Paint by Natasha Collins: Jasmine

HEDGEHOG

SK HD Sugar Modelling Paste: 25g (>¾oz) Beige, 5g (<¼oz) Black and 10g (¼oz) Brown and 5g (<¼oz) White

Floral wire: 22-gauge white

SK Quality Food Colour (QFC) Dusts: Pink

SK Edible Paint by Natasha Collins: Jasmine

CAMPING CAKE

SK Sugarpaste: 1.25kg (2lb 12oz) Bridal White and 1kg (2lb 3¼oz) Lullaby Blue

SK Quality Food Colour (QFC) Paste: Dark Green

SK Professional Paste Food Colour: Vine

Round cake drum: 30.5cm (12")

Round, filled sponge cakes, 12.5cm (5") deep, crumb-coated with buttercream: 12.5cm and 18cm (5" and 7")

CMC cellulose gum

FMM Fluffy Cloud Cutter: small

SK HD Sugar Modelling Paste: 20g (¾oz) Black, 25g (>¾oz) Brown, 330g (11½oz) White and 5g (<¼oz) Summer Yellow

SK Designer Paste Food Colour: Dark Forest

SK Sugar Florist Paste (SFP): 50g (1¾oz) Nasturtium and 5g (<¼oz) White

SK Quality Food Colour (QFC) Dust: Brown

1.5cm (½") width double-faced satin ribbon: 1m (1yd ⅜") pale green

BADGER

1   Combine 10g (¼oz) of black modelling paste with 15g (½oz) of white modelling paste to create a dark grey colour. Roll 20g (¾oz) of dark grey modelling paste into an egg shape. Gradually pinch out one sausage shape from each side of the body for the back legs (A). Flatten the end of each sausage then pinch the tip between your thumb and forefinger. Use a craft knife to mark in the individual toes (B). Indent the pads using a very small ball tool.

2   Roll out a small piece of white modelling paste into an ovoid and fix it to the front of the body using edible glue (C). Use a Dresden tool to mark creases at the top of the back legs.

3   For the front legs, roll two pea-sized balls of dark grey modelling paste into elongated cone shapes and flatten the wider ends slightly. Use a craft knife to mark in the toes on one of the paws and glue it to the left shoulder with the paw against the chest. For the right front leg, use a craft knife to mark in the toes and a ball tool to mark in the pads. Cut a cocktail stick in half and insert it into the leg. Push the cocktail stick into the body so the badger is waving and use edible glue to secure the join (D).

4   For the head, roll 20g (¾oz) of white modelling paste into an ovoid. Tease each end into a point

then push a Dresden tool into the point to divide it in half (E). Use your fingers to soften and shape the points.

5   Push your thumbs into the top of the head to create the eye sockets (F). Use a silicone modelling tool to mark in the mouth and a small ball tool to finish the corners of the smile. Push the wide end of a Dresden tool into the centre of the mouth to open it out then fill it with a small ball of pink modelling paste.

6   Roll two small pieces of dark grey modelling paste into tapered sausage shapes and flatten them slightly. Glue the strips to the face so they run from the eye sockets to the back of the head.

7   To make the ears, flatten a pea-sized ball of dark grey modelling paste, push a large ball tool into the centre then cut the shape in half. Glue the two pieces on top of the head.

8   Push a ball tool into the eye sockets and fill each indentation with a small ball of black modelling paste.

9   For the nose, roll a small capsule shape of black modelling paste and glue it in place on the face. Finish the face with a light dusting of Pink dust food colour over the cheeks. Add highlights to the eyes using Jasmine edible paint applied with a mini ball tool (G).

TOP TIP

These critters are the perfect size to use as cupcake toppers. Roll out a circle of Green modelling paste, add some grass and glue the cuties in the middle.

FOX

1   Roll 25g (<¾oz) of orange modelling paste into an egg shape and flatten the base. Mark in the front legs with a Dresden tool (H). Push away the paste from either side of the legs to accentuate them. Use a silicone modelling tool and Dresden tool to mark the haunches (I).

2   For the front paws, slightly flatten two small balls of brown modelling paste and use a craft knife to mark in the toes. Glue the paws under the front legs. For the back paws, roll two small balls of brown modelling paste into cones, use a craft knife to mark in the toes and glue the narrow ends underneath the haunches.

3   To finish the body, roll a marble-sized piece of white modelling paste into a teardrop and flatten one side. Use a Dresden tool to mark lines in the paste to represent fur. Glue the teardrop shape onto the fox's chest.

4   To make the tail, roll 8g (¼oz) of orange modelling paste into a sausage with tapered ends. Cut away one end and replace it with white modelling paste. Blend the join with your fingers, easing some of the white paste down to create a scalloped pattern (J). Bend the tail and glue it to the back of the body. Use a piece of foam to hold the tip of the tail in place until it is firm.

5   For the fox's head, shape 20g (¾oz) of orange modelling paste into a hemisphere and use your fingers to draw out the muzzle. Lightly press your thumbs into the paste on either side of the muzzle to create the eye sockets. Roll a marble-sized ball of white modelling paste into a capsule

shape. Thin the centre of the capsule then use your fingers to flatten and stretch either end, leaving the centre thicker (K). Place the paste against the face and shape it to fit the eye sockets. Use your fingers to re-shape the muzzle (L). Pinch the cheeks out to a point then use a Dresden tool to split the points in half before defining them with your fingers.

6 Draw in the mouth with a silicon modelling tool. Add a small triangle of brown modelling paste to the muzzle for the nose. Push a ball tool into the eye sockets and fill the indentations with small balls of black modelling paste.

7 For the ears, shape two pea-sized pieces of orange modelling paste into cones. Flatten the cones slightly then use a cone tool to hollow out the inner ear. Fill the inner ear with a small cone of white modelling paste and use the cone tool to re-shape it. Trim away the wide end of each ear and glue them on either side of the head. Brush the cheeks and inner ears with Pink dust food colour. Add highlights to the eyes using Jasmine edible paint.

HEDGEHOG

1 Roll a 20g (¾oz) ball of beige modelling paste into an egg shape. Use the side of your finger to mark a groove halfway along the body. Use your fingers to extrude the nose and muzzle from the narrower end of the body (M).

2 Use a silicone modelling tool to mark the mouth beneath the nose and a very small ball tool to finish the corners of the smile. Gently push a medium ball tool into the face on either side of the nose to form the eye sockets and smooth away any harsh lines with your fingers. Use a ball tool to mark the eyes and create two holes on the top of the head for the ears.

3 Fill the eye holes with small balls of black modelling paste. Roll two small cone shapes of beige modelling paste and insert the narrow ends into the holes on top of the head to form the ears. Push a small ball tool into the centre of each ear and pull it down towards the head to create the inner ears. Roll a small cone of brown modelling paste and attach it to the tip of the muzzle to make the nose.

4 To create the spines, flatten 8g (¼oz) of brown modelling paste and glue it to the back of the body (N). Use a Dresden tool to draw lines in the surface of the paste (O). Roll two small pieces of brown modelling paste into cones and glue them to the forehead.

5 To make the marshmallow and twig, roll a pea-sized ball of brown modelling paste into a 2cm (¾") long sausage. Cut a 22-gauge floral wire to a 3cm (1⅛") length, dip it in edible glue and insert through the sausage, leaving 3mm (⅛") protruding at one end and 8mm (¼") at the other. Cut into the side of the sausage to create a branch then use a Dresden tool to draw lines along the length of the twig (P). Repeat this step to create a second wired twig.

6 For the marshmallows, roll four small pieces of white modelling paste into cylinders. Attach one marshmallow to the end of the shorter wire on each twig, setting the other two aside. Lightly brush the marshmallows on the twigs with Brown dust food colour. Insert the wire at the end of

one twig into the left side of the hedgehog's body.

7 Flatten two balls of beige modelling paste into teardrops and glue them to the chest to create the front paws, wrapping the left hand around the end of the twig. For the back paws, flatten two pea-sized balls of beige modelling paste and use a craft knife to mark in the toes (Q). Glue the paws to the bottom of the body.

8 To finish, lightly dust the hedgehog's cheeks with Pink dust food colour. Add two small highlights to the eyes using Jasmine edible paint.

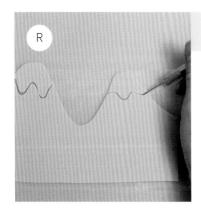

COVERING

1   Colour 1kg (2lb ¾oz) of Bridal White sugarpaste light green using Dark Green and Vine paste food colours. Use 500g (1lb 1¾oz) of the green-coloured sugarpaste to cover the cake drum (see page 30).

2   Use a Dresden tool to mark groups of three short lines in the surface of the sugarpaste to represent blades of grass.

3   Knead 250g (8¾oz) of Bridal White sugarpaste into 1kg (2lb 3¼oz) of Lullaby Blue sugarpaste. Use 750g (1lb 10½oz) of light blue sugarpaste to cover the 18cm (7") cake and 500g (1lb 1¾oz) of light blue sugarpaste to cover the 12.5cm (5") cake (see page 28). Set the covered cakes aside to firm for 24 hours.

4   Once firm, secure the 18cm (7") cake to the back of the covered cake drum using royal icing. Dowel and stack the cakes (see page 31).

SIDE DECORATION

1   Knead ½tsp of CMC into the remaining green-coloured sugarpaste. Wrap the paste well with cling film and set it aside for two hours.

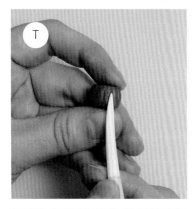

2   Roll the strengthened green paste out to a 2mm (¹⁄₁₆") thickness and cut out a 7.5cm x 59cm (3" x 23") strip. Lightly grease a strip of baking parchment with white vegetable fat and lay the sugarpaste strip upside down on top. Use a cutting wheel

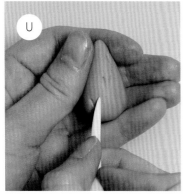

to straighten the bottom edge so it lines up with the bottom of the paper, then cut the top into a wavy line to create rolling hills and mountains. Brush edible glue over the back of the sugarpaste. Use the baking parchment to lift the strip up and apply it to the side of the bottom tier.

3   Repeat step 2 to create the backdrop for the top tier, this time cutting out a 7.5cm x 42cm (3" x 16½") strip. Before attaching the strip, cut away the peaks of some of the mountains in a wavy line and place the cut-away pieces to one side (R). Glue the back of the strip and attach it to the side of the cake. Roll out 20g (¾oz) of white modelling paste to a 2mm (¹⁄₁₆") thickness. Use the cut-away mountain tops as a guide to cut out snowy peaks from the white modelling paste and glue them in place on the cake (S).

4   Use a Dresden tool to mark groups of three short lines on the green areas on each tier. Roll some of the remaining green-coloured paste into long sausage shapes and glue one around the base of each cake.

5   Roll out 25g (>¾oz) of white modelling paste to a 1mm (<¹⁄₁₆") thickness and use the small cloud cutter to cut out six clouds. Fix the clouds to the side of the cake using edible glue.

TOP TIP

Add more depth to the cake by airbrushing the base of the mountains, covered drum and trees with various Green airbrush colours and the tent with Orange liquid colour.

TREES

1   For the trees trunks, divide 25g (>¾oz) of brown modelling paste into 15 pieces: seven small and eight large. Roll each piece into a squat cylinder and use a Dresden tool to draw lines in the sides to mimic bark (T). Set the trunks aside to firm for one hour.

2   To make the pale green trees, colour 150g (5¼oz) of white modelling paste using a combination of Dark Green and Vine paste food colours. Divide the modelling paste into six pieces: one 10g (¼oz), one 20g (¾oz) and four 30g (1oz). Roll each piece into a cone shape. Flatten the backs of the small cone and two of the large cones. Use a Dresden tool to mark small V shapes over the surface of each tree (U). Glue the small flat-backed tree to the back of the top tier, fixing one of the smaller trunks underneath. Attach one of the large flat-backed trees to the back of the bottom tier and the other to the left side.

3   To make the mid-green trees, colour 65g (2¼oz) of white modelling paste with Dark Forest and Vine paste food colours. Divide the paste into four pieces: three 10g (¼oz) and one 35g (1¼oz), and roll them into cones. Mark small V shapes over the surface of the trees.

4   To make the dark green trees, colour 90g (3oz) of white modelling paste using just Dark Forest paste food colour. Divide the paste into five balls: three 10g (¼oz) and two 30g (1oz), and roll them into cones. Flatten the backs of one small and one large cone. Attach the small tree to the back of the top tier and the large tree to the front right of the bottom tier.

TOP TIP

You can swap the icing used in the centre of the tent for RKT (Rice Krispie Treats) or a polystyrene block that you cut to shape.

5   Insert a cocktail stick into each of the remaining trunks and place a tree over the top of each one, fixing it to the trunk with edible glue. Use edible glue to attach the trunks to the cake and drum (V).

TENT

1   Cut out a triangular prism of Bridal White sugarpaste 7cm (2¾") long, 5.5cm (2¼") wide at the base and 6.5cm (2½") tall. Roll out 20g (¾oz) of black modelling paste into a thin sheet and cut out a triangle the same size as the end of the prism. Glue the triangle to the front of the tent.

2   Roll out 10g (¼oz) of Nasturtium SFP into a thin sheet and cut out two triangles the same size as the end of the prism. Glue one to the back of the tent. Cut the other in half and glue it in place at the front of the tent, covering the black triangle. Use your fingers to curl the paste at the base of the door outwards (W).

3   Roll out the remaining Nasturtium SFP into a thin sheet and cut out a 7.5cm x 13.5cm (3" x 5¼") rectangle. Lay the rectangle over the top of the tent and fix it in place using edible glue. Use a Dresden tool to mark a crease along the top of the tent. Use a very small ball tool to mark three evenly spaced holes along each side of the tent (X). Trim the back right corner of the tent to allow it to sit flush

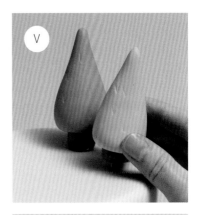

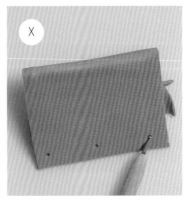

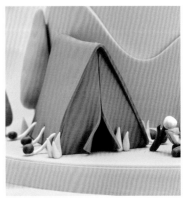

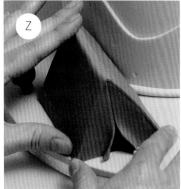

against the side of the cake and fix it in place on the cake drum using edible glue (Y, Z).

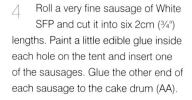

4   Roll a very fine sausage of White SFP and cut it into six 2cm (¾") lengths. Paint a little edible glue inside each hole on the tent and insert one of the sausages. Glue the other end of each sausage to the cake drum (AA).

5   Roll six tiny pieces of brown modelling paste into balls and flatten them into discs. Glue one disc to the end of each sausage.

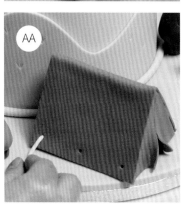

FIRE

1   Divide 5g (<¼oz) of brown modelling paste into five uneven balls and roll each one into a sausage shape. Use a Dresden tool to draw lines in the paste to mimic bark. Use edible glue to fix the logs into a stack at the front of the cake drum.

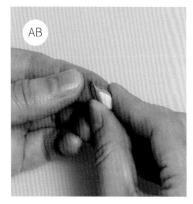

2   To make the flames, roll four very small pieces of yellow modelling paste into teardrops. Shape four slightly larger pieces of orange modelling paste into teardrops. Place the yellow teardrops on top of the orange ones and gently press down to adhere. Finally, shape four slightly

larger teardrops of Nasturtium SFP and place the orange and yellow flame on top. Gently press down to adhere (AB). Glue the flames in and around the logs.

3   Stick the remaining marshmallows next to the fire and insert the wired twig into the drum with the marshmallow over the fire.

FINISHING TOUCHES

1   Use edible glue to fix the animals in place on the cake and drum. Glue clusters of three small cones of green modelling paste around the decorations on the cake drum.

2   Wrap pale green ribbon around the edge of the cake drum and fix it in place with double-sided tape.

TOP TIP

Cut out an oblong and roll two sausages from Brown modelling paste. Add woodgrain texture to each piece with the dresden tool. Leave to dry overnight and then use a Black edible ink pen to write your special message. Glue the sign post to the front of the cake.

BABY ANIMALS

What's even cuter than regular animals? Baby animals! These characters are all made using simple shapes and similar techniques so once you've mastered one, you can make them all.

HIPPO

SK HD Sugar Modelling Paste: 5g (<¼oz) Black and 125g (4½oz) White

SK Professional Paste Food Colour: Thrift

ELEPHANT

SK HD Sugar Modelling Paste: 5g (<¼oz) Black, 5g (<¼oz) Blue and 160g (5½oz) White

LION

SK HD Sugar Modelling Paste: 100g (3½oz) Beige, 5g (<¼oz) Black, 5g (<¼oz) Brown and 10g (¼oz) White

SK Professional Paste Food Colours: Rose and Teddy Bear Brown

MONKEY

SK HD Sugar Modelling Paste: 5g (<¼oz) Black, 60g (2oz) Brown and 50g (1¾oz) White

Heart-shaped cutter: 2.5cm (1")

ALLIGATOR

SK HD Sugar Modelling Paste: 5g (<¼oz) Black, 50g (1¾oz) Green, 5g (<¼oz) White and 5g (<¼oz) Yellow

SK Professional Paste Food Colour: Sunflower

JUNGLE CAKE

SK Sugarpaste: 750g (1lb 10½oz) Bridal White, 50g (1¾oz) Magical Blue and 400g (14oz) Palm Green

Round, filled sponge cake, 10cm (4") deep, crumb coated with buttercream: 15cm (6")

Round cake drum: 30.5cm (12")

Round cake card: 15cm (6")

SK HD Sugar Modelling Paste: 125g (4½oz) Green

1.5cm (½") width satin ribbon: 1m (1yd 3⅜") pale blue

HIPPO

1   Colour 112g (<4oz) of white modelling paste purple using Thrift paste food colour.

2   Roll 55g (2oz) of the purple modelling paste into an egg shape and lay it on its side. Divide 20g (¾oz) of purple modelling paste into four balls. Roll each ball into a cylinder with one end wider than the other. Use a small ball tool to mark three indentations in the wider end of each leg (A). Fill each indentation with a tiny ball of white modelling paste to make the toes. Use edible glue to attach the legs to the left side of the body. For the legs on the right side, which will be elevated, insert a 2cm (¾") length of cocktail stick into the narrower end of each leg before pushing the other end into the body (B). This will provide extra support. Press a small ball tool into the body to create the belly button.

3   Roll 35g (1¼oz) of purple modelling paste into an egg shape. Press your fingers into the top of the egg to create the eye sockets (C). Use a medium ball tool to create a well in the centre of each socket (D).

4   Colour 12g (>¼oz) of white modelling paste with slightly less Thrift paste food colour than before to create a pale purple paste. Roll 10g (¼oz) of the pale purple modelling paste into an ovoid and flatten the back. Create two indentations in the front of the ovoid using a small ball tool then gently push the ball tool upwards to stretch the paste slightly and open out the nostrils (E). Use the broad end of a Dresden tool to further enhance the nostrils. Glue the snout in place at the front of the head. Roll

the remaining pale purple paste into a sausage with tapered ends and glue it along the bottom edge of the ovoid. Use the pointed end of a Dresden tool to continue the smile onto the ovoid then press a small ball tool into each end to make dimples (F).

5   Fill each eye socket with a small ball of white modelling paste. Press a ball tool into the top edge of each eye and fill each well with a small ball of black modelling paste. Roll a very fine sausage of black modelling paste, cut it in half and glue one piece around the top of each eye. Finish each eye with a small ball of White modelling paste.

6   Roll out a small piece of white modelling paste and cut out two tiny rectangles. Glue the teeth inside the mouth.

7   Press a ball tool into the top of the head to create holes for the ears. Roll two small cones of purple modelling paste and press the broad end of a Dresden tool into the front of each one to shape the inner ears (G). Pinch the narrow end of each ear to a point and glue the points inside the holes created in the head.

8   Use edible glue to attach the hippo's head to the body.

ELEPHANT

1   Knead small amounts of blue and black modelling paste into 150g (5¼oz) of white modelling paste to create a pale blue/grey colour.

2   Roll 55g (2oz) of pale blue/grey modelling paste into an egg shape and flatten the widest end.

Use the pointed end of a Dresden tool to draw creases in the sides of the body. Add a belly button using a small ball tool.

3   Divide 10g (¼oz) of pale blue/grey modelling paste in half and roll each piece into a cylinder with one end wider than the other. Use a small ball tool to mark three indentations in the wider end of each leg then fill each indentation with a tiny ball of white modelling paste to make the toes. Use edible glue to attach one leg to each side of the body.

4   For the front legs, roll 10g (¼oz) of pale blue/grey modelling paste into a long cone shape and flatten the wider end. Use a sharp knife to trim one edge of the cone flat, thinning the pointed end even further (H). Glue the cut edge to the front of the body (I). Add the toes in the same way as for the rear legs. Repeat to create a second leg.

5   Roll a small ball of pale blue/grey modelling paste into a long, thin sausage shape with a tapered end. Glue the tail to the back of the elephant.

6   Roll 55g (2oz) of pale blue/grey modelling paste into a ball then extrude a trunk shape pinch the paste on one side (J). The tip of the trunk should be narrower than the base.

7   Press your thumbs into the face on either side of the trunk to create the eye sockets (K). Press a ball tool into the inner edge of each socket to around a 5mm (¼") depth.

8   Press a small ball tool into the tip of the trunk and rock it

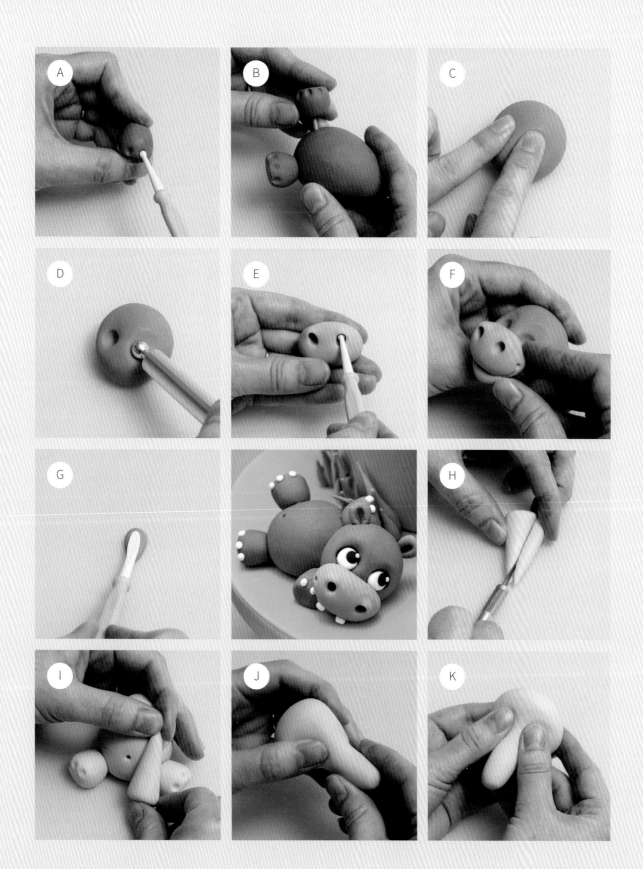

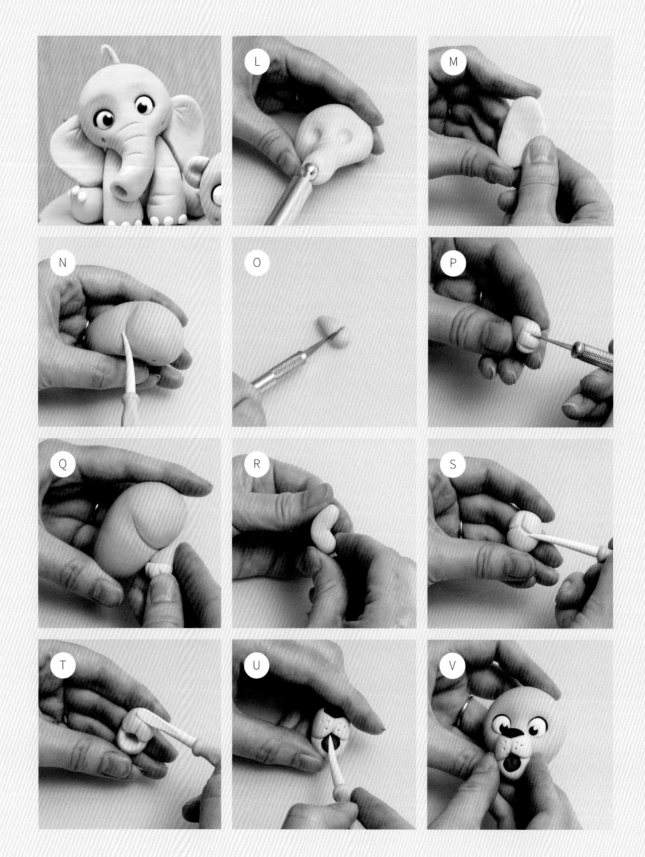

from side to side to open out the hole (L). Pinch the tip of the trunk into a triangular shape. Gently bend the trunk downwards. Use a scribing tool to draw horizontal lines across the base of the trunk.

9   Use the pointed end of a Dresden tool to draw the edges of a smile on each side of the trunk. Finish each line with a small indentation created with a mini ball tool.

10   Fill each eye socket with a small ball of white modelling paste. Press a ball tool into the inner edge of each eye and fill each well with a small ball of black modelling paste. Roll a very fine sausage of black modelling paste, cut it in half and glue one piece around the top of each eye. Finish each eye with a small ball of white modelling paste.

11   Use edible glue to attach the elephant's head to its body.

12   Place a 4g (<¼oz) ball of pale blue/grey modelling paste in the palm of your hand. Lightly press the paste with the palm of your opposite hand to stretch and shape it into a flat ear shape (M). Repeat with a second ball to make the opposite ear. Glue the ears in place on either side of the head.

LION

1   Add a little Teddy Bear Brown paste food colour to 100g (3½oz) of beige modelling paste to make a golden brown tone. Colour 10g (¼oz) of white modelling paste with Teddy Bear Brown paste food colour to create a pale brown tone.

2   Roll 50g (1¾oz) of the golden-brown modelling paste into an egg shape and gently elongate it. Press the side of your finger into the side of the shape approximately halfway along to create the haunches, then repeat on the other side of the body. Use the pointed end of a Dresden tool to enhance the crease between the haunches and the body (N).

3   Roll two large-pea-sized balls of golden-brown modelling paste into cone shapes and cut off the wider ends (O). Replace the cut-away pieces of paste with pale brown paste. Use the pointed end of a Dresden tool to mark in the toes then deepen the lines with a craft knife (P). Glue the hind legs underneath the haunches (Q).

4   For the front legs, roll two marble-sized balls of golden brown modelling paste into sausage shapes with one wider end. Bend each leg in the centre (R). Cut away the wider ends and replace the cut-away pieces with pale brown modelling paste. Repeat step 3 to shape the toes. Glue one front leg to each side of the body, positioning the left paw further forward than the right.

5   Push a small ball tool into the back of the lion's body. Roll a small, tapered sausage of golden brown modelling paste and bend it into a curve. Glue the wider end of the sausage into the hole and use food grade foam to support it in position until it holds its own weight.

6   Roll 40g (1½oz) of golden brown modelling paste into an ovoid. Use the side of your hand to mark a groove across the eye area. Push a ball tool into the groove to create two eye sockets.

7   Fill each eye socket with a small ball of white modelling paste. Press a ball tool into the inner edge of each eye and fill each well with a small ball of black modelling paste. Roll a very fine sausage of black modelling paste, cut it in half and glue one piece around the top of each eye. Finish each eye with a small ball of white modelling paste.

8   For the muzzle, shape 4g (<¼oz) of pale brown modelling paste into an ovoid and flatten the back to create a domed shape. Use the pointed end of a Dresden tool to draw three lines in the front of the shape to create the mouth (S). Push the broad end of a Dresden tool into the paste just underneath the mouth and gently pull it down and away to open out the smile. Press the tool across the top of the muzzle to create a shallow dent where the nose will sit (T). Shape a very small ball of black modelling paste into an elongated triangle and glue it inside the dent. Use a small ball tool or cocktail stick to indent three dots on either side of the muzzle for the whiskers. Fill the open mouth with a small sheet of black modelling paste, using the Dresden tool to help push the paste into place. Colour a tiny piece of white modelling paste pink using Rose paste food colour. Roll the paste into a cone and glue it inside the mouth, flattening it into place. Use the pointed end of a Dresden tool to draw a line down the centre of the tongue (U).

9   Use edible glue to attach the muzzle to the front of the face (V). Use the pointed end of a Dresden tool to continue the lines of the smile onto the rest of the face, curving them up towards the eyes. Finish each line with an indentation created with a mini ball tool.

10 Roll a marble-sized ball of golden brown modelling paste into a capsule shape and flatten it with your fingers. Press the broad end of a Dresden tool into the centre of the paste to create a well. Cut the capsule shape in half and neaten the cut edges with your fingers. Glue the ears in place on either side of the head.

11 Use edible glue to fix the head to the body. Once the tail has set firm, roll a small piece of brown modelling paste into a cone and glue it to the tip.

MONKEY

1 Knead together 55g (2oz) of brown modelling paste and 30g (1oz) of white modelling paste to create a light brown tone. Add small pinches of brown modelling paste to 15g (½oz) of white modelling paste to create a beige colour.

2 Roll 25g (>¾oz) of light brown modelling paste into an egg shape. Pinch a large-pea-sized ball of beige-coloured modelling paste to flatten it, then stretch the paste into an oval. Glue the oval to the front of the egg shape and use your fingers to smooth and blend the joins (W). Press a small ball tool into the egg to create a belly button.

3 Roll 5g (<¼oz) of light brown modelling paste into a long, thin sausage shape and trim it to a 5cm (2") length. Bend the sausage into a loose curl and set it aside to firm.

4 Roll 4g (<¼oz) of pale brown modelling paste into a 4cm (1½") long sausage. Bend the sausage to a right angle halfway along its length (X).

Repeat to create a second leg. Glue the legs to either side of the body so the bend points outwards on each side. Glue the tail to the back of the body, supporting it until it can hold its own weight.

5 Flatten two pea-sized balls of beige-coloured modelling paste into chunky discs. Pinch out one side of each disc to form teardrop shapes. Use a Dresden tool to create three toes in the rounded side of each shape then enhance the indentations with a craft knife (Y). Glue one foot at the end of each leg (Z).

6 Repeat steps 4–5 to make two arms, this time cutting the sausages of paste to the same length as the body. Glue one arm to each shoulder with the left arm hanging at the side of the body and the right arm resting on the monkey's lap.

7 Roll 35g (1¼oz) of light brown modelling paste into a ball. Use the side of your hand to mark a groove across the eye area. Roll out a small piece of beige-coloured modelling paste into a thin sheet and cut out a heart using the 2.5cm (1") heart cutter. Glue the shape over the face, positioning the top of the heart in the groove. Push a ball tool into each side of the face to create the eye sockets (AA).

8 Shape 5g (<¼oz) of beige-coloured modelling paste into an ovoid wide enough to cover the bottom half of the face and flatten the back. Glue the muzzle to the face just below the eyes. Use a small ball tool to indent the nostrils in the front of the muzzle. Use the pointed end of a Dresden tool to draw a smiling mouth in the base of the muzzle (AB). Add a dimple to each end of the smile using a small ball tool.

9 Fill each eye socket with a small ball of white modelling paste. Press a ball tool into the inner edge of each eye and fill each well with a small ball of black modelling paste. Roll a very fine sausage of black modelling paste, cut it in half and glue one piece around the top of each eye. Finish each eye with a small ball of white modelling paste.

10 For the ears, roll a large-pea-sized ball of beige modelling paste and press a large ball tool into the surface, pulling it over to one side (AC). Pinch the paste on either side of the well together to create a point (AD). Push a ball tool into either side of the head to create two indentations (AE). Brush a little edible glue inside each hole then insert the pointed ends of the ears (AF). Use a ball tool to press the ear into the head.

11 Glue the monkey's head on top of its body. Add a small curl of light brown modelling paste on top of the head.

ALLIGATOR

1 Knead a little Sunflower paste food colour into 45g (1½oz) of green modelling paste to create a vibrant green tone.

2 Roll 5g (<¼oz) of vibrant green modelling paste into a cone. Flatten the wider end and bend the tip backwards a little to add a gentle curve. Use the broad end of a Dresden tool to create a triangular well in the outer edge of the curve (AG). Glue a small piece of yellow modelling paste inside the well and gently flatten it into the cone with your fingers. Use the pointed end of a Dresden tool

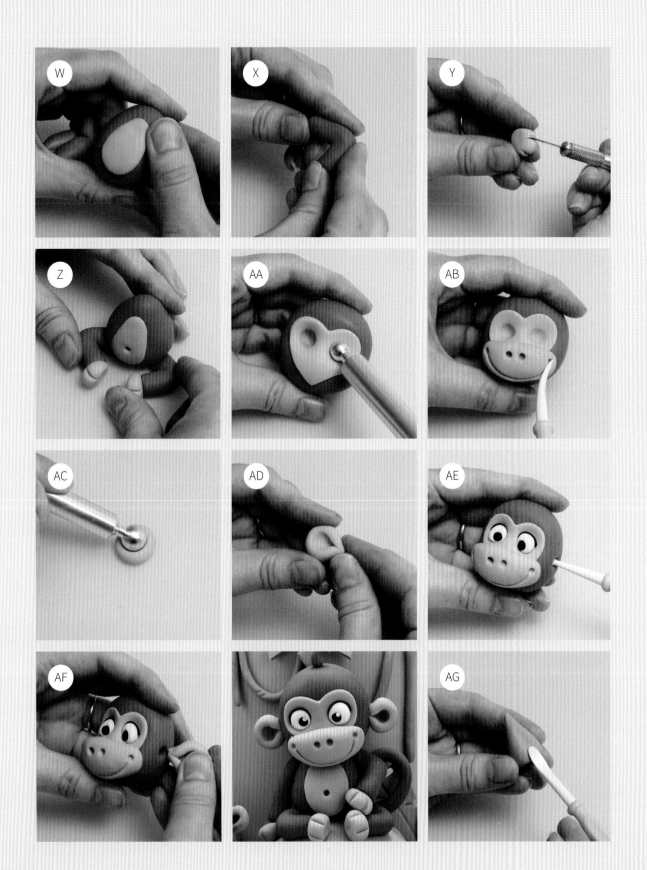

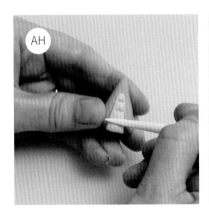

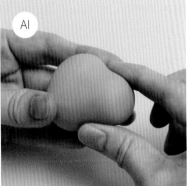

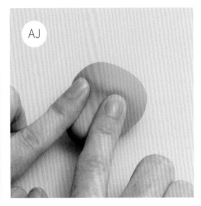

to mark horizontal lines across the yellow section (AH). Roll four small pieces of green modelling paste into cone shapes and attach them in a line along the opposite side of the tail. Use edible glue to attach the tail to your chosen cake or display board.

3 Shape 40g (1½oz) of vibrant green modelling paste into a ball. Pinch and roll one side of the ball to extrude a sausage shape for the snout (AI). Press your fingers or a large ball tool into the paste just above the snout to indent the eye sockets (AJ). Place the side of your finger over the top of the head and gently press down to shape the skull. Flatten the end of the snout and add two indentations for the nostrils using a ball tool. Use a scribing tool to mark three horizontal lines over the top of

the snout. Use the pointed end of a Dresden tool to draw a smiling mouth in the front of the snout (AK). Add a dimple at either end of the mouth using a small ball tool.

4 Press a medium ball tool into the base of each eye socket to create wells for the eyes (AL). Fill the eye sockets with two small balls of white modelling paste. Press a ball tool into the bottom edge of each eye and fill each well with a small ball of black modelling paste. Roll a very fine sausage of black modelling paste, cut it in half and glue one piece around the top of each eye (AM). Finish each eye with a small ball of white modelling paste for the highlight.

5 Roll two small pieces of White modelling paste into triangular

shapes and attach one to each side of the face, lining up the base with the lower lip.

6 Roll three small pieces of green modelling paste into cone shapes. Glue the cones in a row running along the back of the head. Glue the head to the cake or board approximately 4cm (1½") in front of the tail.

TOP TIP

If you want to add a name to the cake, try painting the name into the water using Jasmine(White) edible paint and a 00 paintbrush. You can add some wavy lines to look like lapping water too.

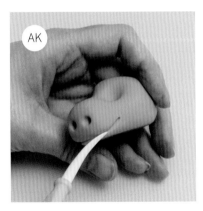

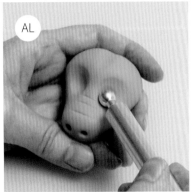

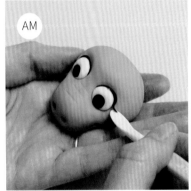

COVERING

1　Knead 50g (1¾oz) of Magical Blue sugarpaste into 450g (1lb) of Bridal White sugarpaste to create a mid-blue colour.

2　Use the mid-blue sugarpaste to cover the cake drum (see page 30). Set the covered drum aside to firm overnight.

3　Knead together 300g (10½oz) of Bridal White sugarpaste and 400g (14oz) of Palm Green sugarpaste to make a pale green colour. Use the pale green sugarpaste to cover the cake (see page 28).

DECORATIONS

1　Spread 15g (½oz) of royal icing towards the back of the covered cake drum and place the cake on top.

2　Divide 35g (1¼oz) of green modelling paste into 30 balls and roll each ball into a long cone. Group the cones together into eight clusters and use edible glue to fix them around the base of the cake.

3　Roll 10g (¼oz) of green modelling paste into a long, thin sausage. Drape lengths of the sausage around the top edge of the cake to represent vines and glue them in place.

4　Roll out 30g (1oz) of green modelling paste to a 2mm (¹/₁₆") thickness and cut out 12 leaf shapes. Use a sharp craft knife to cut out small

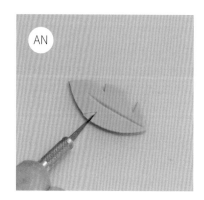

triangles from the sides of the leaves (AN). Group the leaves into five clusters and fix them around the base of the cake using edible glue.

5　Knead a small pinch of CMC into 30g (1oz) of pale green sugarpaste. Shape the paste into a mound and glue it against the front edge of the cake, positioning it centrally.

6　Wrap pale blue ribbon around the edge of the cake drum and fix it in place with double-sided tape.

MODELS

1　Use edible glue to attach the elephant to the top left side of the cake and the lion to the right.

2　Glue the monkey on top of the mound at the front of the cake.

3　Glue the hippo towards the left side of the cake drum and the alligator's head and tail on the right side of the drum, making sure they are in line with one another.

PRIDE OF LIONS

This playful daddy lion and his young cubs is great for Father's Day or even a safari-themed birthday party. This isn't on a cake but would look great with the safari design on page 143.

SEATED LION

SK HD Sugar Modelling Paste: 5g (<¼oz) Black, 5g (<¼oz) Brown and 75g (<2½oz) White

SK Professional Paste Food Colour: Marigold

Blade tool

ADULT LION

SK HD Sugar Modelling Paste: 5g (<¼oz) Black, 65g (2^1/$_3$oz) Brown and 260g (<9¼oz) White

SK Professional Paste Food Colour: Chestnut and Marigold

CLIMBING CUB

SK HD Sugar Modelling Paste: 5g (<¼oz) Black, 5g (<¼oz) Brown and 35g (1¼oz) White

SK Professional Paste Food Colour: Berberis and Marigold

SEATED LION CUB

1   Colour 60g (2oz) of white modelling paste with Marigold paste food colour to make a golden tone. Colour 10g (¼oz) of white modelling paste with a very small amount of Marigold paste food colour for a paler tone.

2   Roll 35g (1¼oz) of the golden modelling paste into an egg shape then flatten the wider end to create a base for the model to sit on.

3   Roll a small-pea-sized ball of the pale golden modelling paste into a cone then gently pinch and flatten it. Use a little edible glue to attach the paste to the front of the egg and, with fingers greased with white vegetable fat, smooth the edges of the paste to soften the join (A).

4   To mark the front legs, push the flat side of a blade tool into the centre of the paler paste, with the point facing down (B). Use the blade tool to mark the outer edge of each leg then use your fingers to smooth away any harsh lines. Mark the haunches on either side of the body using a Dresden tool (C).

5   For the paws, roll four pea-sized balls of golden modelling paste. Lightly pinch two of the balls into thick discs then push a craft knife into the end of each disc twice to form the toes (D). Glue the two paws under the legs at the front of the cub's body. Roll the remaining two balls into cone shapes and use the craft knife to mark two toes at the wider end of the cones. Glue the paws underneath the haunches (E).

6   Combine the remaining pale golden modelling paste with an

equal quantity of white modelling paste to make an even paler tone. Roll a small ball of this paste into a cone and flatten it a little. Push a Dresden tool into the paste twice on either side to create the fur (F). Use your fingers to shape the edges into points. Fix the fur to the chest with edible glue.

7   For the head, roll 20g (¾oz) of golden modelling paste into an ovoid. Use the side of your hand to mark a groove through the centre for the eye area (G). Push a large ball tool into the paste on either side of the groove to form the eye sockets (H). Use your fingers to smooth away any harsh lines. Push a smaller ball tool into the centre of the eye sockets (I). Lightly smooth away any harsh lines, taking care not to lose the shape. Finally, push a very small ball tool into the eye sockets to create the space for the eyeballs.

8   To make the muzzle, roll two pea-sized balls of pale golden modelling paste and lightly flatten one

into a hemisphere. Roll the other ball into a capsule shape and lightly flatten it with your fingers. Use a Dresden tool to mark a central line down the capsule shape (J). Use a little edible glue to attach the flat side of the hemisphere under the central line of the capsule (K). Shape a very small ball of brown modelling paste into a wide triangle. Attach it to the top of the muzzle with edible glue. Use a cocktail stick to mark whiskers in the cheeks. Secure the muzzle to the head with edible glue.

9   For the eyes, roll two very small balls of white modelling paste and glue them into the eye sockets. Push a small ball tool into the top left corner of each eye and fill the holes with tiny balls of brown modelling paste. Repeat using a smaller ball tool and fill the well with black modelling paste. Add a very tiny dot of white modelling paste to the pupil for a highlight (L).

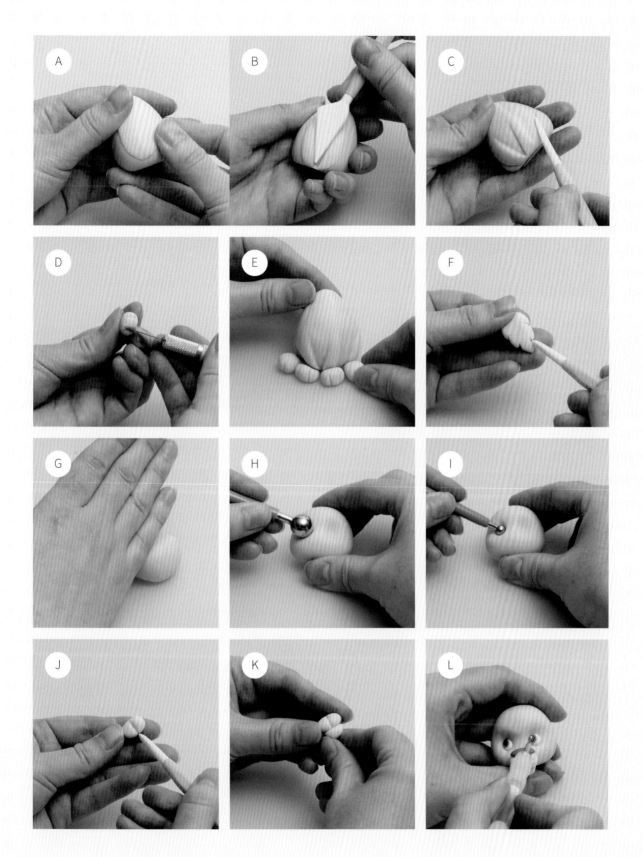

10 To make the ears, flatten two large pea-sized balls of golden modelling paste into thick discs and use a modelling tool to indent the inner ear. Lightly pinch one edge of each ear to create a soft point then trim the point to create a flat edge. Glue the ears on top of the head (M).

11 Add two small cones of golden modelling paste to the top of the head. Push a cocktail stick into the neck, brush a little edible glue on the top of the body and secure the head in place. Set the cub aside to firm.

ADULT LION

1 Colour 250g (<8¾oz) of white modelling paste with Marigold and Chestnut paste food colours to create a warm beige tone. Roll 150g (5¼oz) warm beige modelling paste into a pear shape then flatten the wider end to create a base. Push the narrow top of the shape forwards a little to create an almost flat front.

2 Use a silicone-tipped tool to mark both sides of one front leg on the front of the body (N). Lightly grease your fingers with white vegetable fat and begin to work the paste away from the lines, leaving the leg sitting proud from the body (O). Only one front leg is needed as the other will be added later. Use a Dresden tool to mark the haunches and define the front leg (P).

3 Repeat step 5 from the Seated Lion Cub instructions to make one front paw and two rear paws. Attach the paws under the body with edible glue. Insert a cocktail stick into the neck and leave the model to firm for six hours.

4 For the head, shape a 60g (2oz) ball of warm beige modelling paste into a hemisphere. Use the side of your hand to mark a groove through the eye area. Repeat steps 7 and 9 from the seated lion cub instructions to create the eye sockets and add the eyes, this time facing the eyes towards the nose.

5 Elongate and flatten two large-pea-sized balls of warm beige modelling paste. Shape the ears as for the seated lion cub then glue them in position on either side of the head.

6 For the muzzle, combine a marble-sized ball of warm beige modelling paste with the same quantity of white modelling paste. Split the paste in half, roll one piece into a wide capsule shape and lightly flatten it. Use a Dresden tool to mark a line in the centre. Form the second ball into a disc then square off the edges. Use a Dresden tool to curve the disc into a mouth. Glue the mouth piece under the central line in the capsule shape. Shape a small-pea-sized ball of brown modelling paste into a wide triangle and secure it in place on the top of the muzzle. Attach the muzzle to the face using edible glue. Use a cocktail stick to mark holes for the whiskers.

7 Push the head onto the body at a slight angle, securing it with edible glue. Push a Dresden tool into the mouth to open it further (Q). Fix a small piece of pink modelling paste into the open mouth and use the pointed end of a Dresden tool to mark a the crease in the tongue. Roll two tiny cones of white modelling paste and glue them at either side of the open mouth for the teeth. Leave the model to firm overnight.

8 For the mane, flatten a 20g (¾oz) cone of brown modelling paste to create a teardrop shape. Use a Dresden tool to mark fur lines in the paste then glue it onto the back of the head with the point facing downwards (R). Roll a 40g (1½oz) ball of brown modelling paste into a sausage, thinning it slightly at the ends. Lay the sausage on your worktop in a horseshoe shape. Use the side of your hand to flatten the outside edge of the horseshoe and a Dresden tool to mark lines for the fur (S). Brush a line of edible glue around the head, behind the ears and underneath the chin. Gently support the mane whilst fixing it around the head, positioning the wider middle section underneath the chin (T). Trim away any excess from the join on top of the head. Gently flatten the mane between the lion's ears with your fingers to leave a flat surface for the climbing cub, if needed.

9 To make the tail, roll a ball of warm beige modelling paste into a long sausage with a tapered end. Trim the sausage to an 8cm (3⅛") length. Roll a marble-sized ball of brown modelling paste into a teardrop shape. Push a ball tool into the wide end then use a Dresden tool to mark fur lines down the sides of the shape (U). Brush the narrow point of the tail with edible glue then push it into the hole in the teardrop. Shape the tail and glue the flat end to the back of the lion.

10 Roll 8g (¼oz) of beige paste into a tapered sausage shape. Flatten the wider end into a paw and use a craft knife to mark the toes (V). Trim the narrow end to create a flat surface. Glue the flat edge to the lion's chest (W) and hold it in place whilst you

glue the seated lion cub in front. Add a little edible glue to the paw and attach it to the side of the seated cub.

CLIMBING CUB

1   Colour 30g (1oz) of white modelling paste using Marigold and Berberis paste food colours to create a light orange tone. Repeat step 5 from the Seated Lion Cub instructions to make two front paws. Glue the paws on top of the adult lion's mane (X).

2   For the body, roll 15g (½oz) of pale orange modelling paste into an egg shape. Use the side of your finger to narrow the top of the egg (Y). Use edible glue to fix the body to the back of the adult lion's head (Z).

3   To make the back legs, roll two large-pea-sized balls of pale orange modelling paste into 1.5cm (½") long sausages, keeping one end wider for the paw. Use a craft knife to mark the toes (AA). Glue the first leg to the base of the egg shape so it hangs down from the body (AB). Repeat for the second leg, this time bending the leg at the knee and attaching the foot to the back of the lions head, as well as to the cub's body (AC).

4   Roll a very small piece of pale orange modelling paste into a tapered sausage shape approximately 2cm (¾") long. Push a small ball tool into the base of the cub's body and fix the tapered sausage into it, bending it slightly to create a curve in the tail (AD).

5   For the head, roll 10g (¼oz) of pale orange modelling paste into an ovoid and follow steps 7–10 from the Seated Lion Cub instructions, this time facing the eyes inwards. Use edible glue to fix the head on top of the paws (AE).

6   Roll small pieces of brown modelling paste into teardrop shapes and mark fur lines over their surface using a Dresden tool. Use the teardrops to fill out the mane at the back of the lion's head, arranging them on either side of the climbing cub.

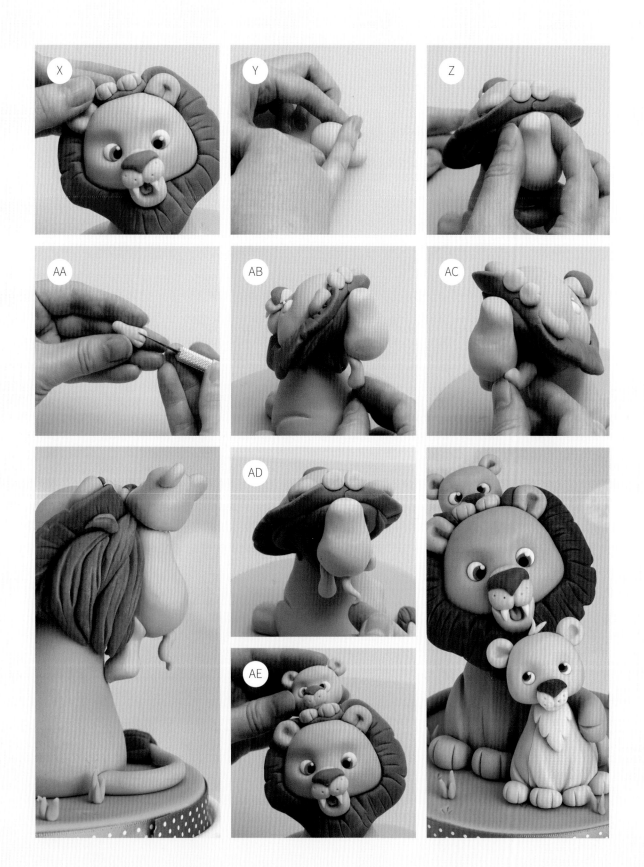

GARDEN GANG

This collection of creepy crawlies and critters is just the thing for anyone who loves getting grubby in the garden. The modelling techniques are all really simple so you can create your own plant pot scene in no time at all.

YOU WILL NEED

FROG

SK HD Sugar Modelling Paste: 75g (2½oz) Green and 15g (½oz) White

SK Professional Paste Food Colour: Leaf Green

Food colour pen: black

SNAIL

SK HD Sugar Modelling Paste: 8g (¼oz) Beige, 15g (½oz) Brown and 5g (<¼oz) White

Food colour pen: black

LADYBIRD

SK HD Sugar Modelling Paste: 5g (<¼oz) Black, 10g (¼oz) Red and 5g (<¼oz) White

Food colour pen: black

SPIDER

SK HD Sugar Modelling Paste: 25g (>¾oz) Black and 5g (<¼oz) White

SK Edible Paint by Natasha Collins: Jasmine

Food colour pen: black

BEETLE

SK HD Sugar Modelling Paste: 20g (¾oz) Black and 8g (¼oz) White

SK Designer Moon Beam Dust Food Colours: Ruby and Sapphire

Food colour pen: black

PLANT POT CAKE

Round cake drum: 25.5cm (10")

SK Sugarpaste: 1.1kg (2lb 6¾oz) Bridal White and 350g (12¼oz) Coco Brown

Round cake cards: 10cm and 15cm (4" and 6")

Round, filled chocolate cake, 12.5cm (5") deep: 15cm (6")

400g (14oz) chocolate buttercream

SK Designer Paste Food Colour: Terracotta

Airbrush kit

SK Professional Liquid Food Colours: Bulrush, Leaf Green and Nasturtium

CMC cellulose gum

PME Oval Cutter: 5cm x 9cm (2" x 3½")

FMM Tappits: Alphabet and Numbers Upper Case

Spider's web template, see page 180

SK Sugar Florist Paste (SFP): 20g (¾oz) White

SK HD Modelling Paste: 5g (<¼oz) Pink, 30g (1oz) Red and 25g (>¾oz) White

PME Daisy Plunger Cutters: 1.3cm and 2cm (½" and ¾")

SK Professional Paste Food Colours: Leaf Green and Sunflower

Cupped flower formers

1.5cm (½") width ribbon satin: 80cm (32") bright green

FROG

1   Roll 35g (1¼oz) of green modelling paste into an egg shape. Lay the shape on its side and carefully flatten the wider end. Pull up the narrower end so that it points upwards. Use the side of your hand to indent a groove down the centre of the back (A).

2   Knead Leaf Green paste food colour into 10g (¼oz) of white modelling paste. Roll small balls of the leaf-green-coloured modelling paste and glue them along the side of the body, pressing them down to flatten them into discs.

3   For the back legs, roll 4g (⅛oz) of green modelling paste into a sausage with a tapered end. Bend the sausage in half and shape the outer edge of the bend to a point to form the knee (B). Glue the leg on one side of the body. Repeat to add a second back leg. Add small balls of leaf-green-coloured modelling paste to each leg.

4   For the back feet, flatten two pea-sized balls of green modelling paste into discs and cut

away two triangles from each foot to form three toes (C). Shape the toes with your fingers. Add a small ball of leaf-green-coloured modelling paste to the tip of each toe. Glue the feet under the back legs.

5   For the front legs, roll 4g (⅛oz) of green modelling paste into a sausage shape. Pinch one end to flatten it into a disc (D). Repeat step 4 to create the toes. Bend the sausage in half and use a Dresden tool to add creases around the bend. Glue the leg to the front of the body (E). Repeat to add the final leg.

6   To make the head, roll 20g (¾oz) of green modelling paste into an egg shape and flatten one side. Use a Dresden tool to draw a mouth across the front of the shape. Run the wide end of a Dresden tool around the bottom of the mouth to accentuate the chin (F). Use your fingers to smooth and shape the chin and neck. Push a small ball tool into either side of the smile to finish the mouth. Push a small ball tool into the front of the face, above the mouth to form the nostrils.

7   Push a large ball tool into the top of the head to create indentations for the eye sockets (G). Roll two pea-sized pieces of white modelling paste into balls and use edible glue to fix them into the eye sockets. Use a black edible ink pen to draw in the pupils. Shape a pea-sized ball of green modelling paste into a sausage with tapered ends. Gently flatten the shape and fix it behind the eyeballs using edible glue. Use a Dresden tool to help fit the paste around the eyes (H).

8   Push a cocktail stick into frog's neck and push the head in onto it, securring with edible glue.

SNAIL

1   Roll 8g (¼oz) of beige modelling paste into an elongated cone (I). Push the handle of a paintbrush into the wider end of the cone to make an indentation. Use your fingers to pinch and roll the paste on each side of the indentation to create the two tentacles for the eyes (J).

2   Bend the cone at a right angle approximately one third of the way along its length (K). Gently flatten the larger section. Push a scallop tool into the paste just below the tentacles to make the mouth (L).

3   For the shell, roll a 15g (½oz) piece of brown modelling paste into an elongated cone. Roll the cone into a spiral, starting from the tip (M). Glue the shell on top of the body.

4   Roll two small balls of white modelling paste and glue one on top of each tentacle. Finish by drawing a small dot in the centre of each eye using a black edible ink pen.

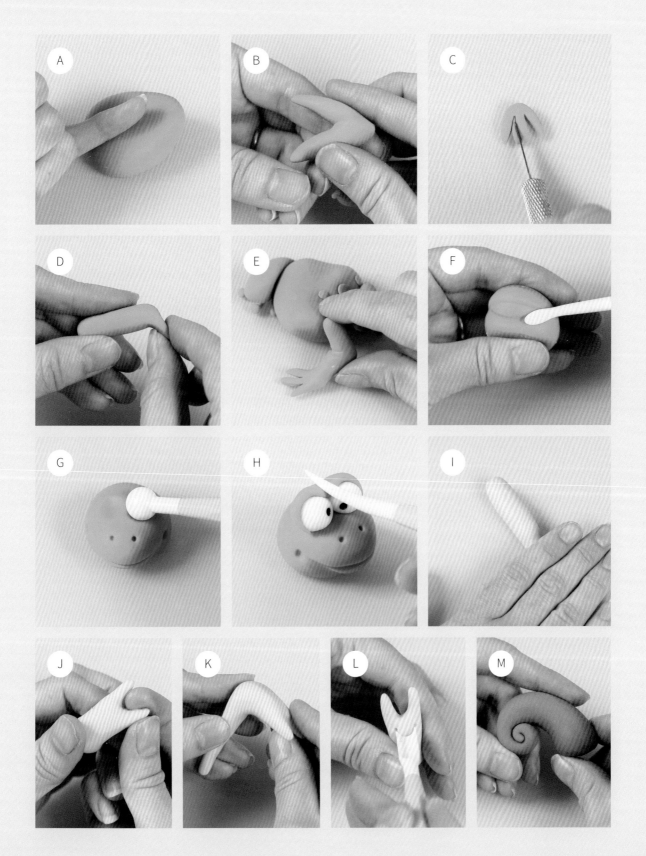

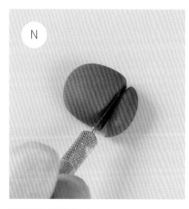

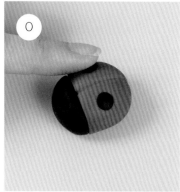

LADYBIRD

1   Roll 10g (¼oz) of red modelling paste into an ovoid. Use a sharp knife to trim away one third of the shape at the end of the ovoid (N). Replace the cut-away piece with black modelling paste.

2   Use a Dresden tool to draw a line along the centre of the ladybird's back. Push the small end of a ball tool into the face to indent the eye sockets and use a scallop tool to mark the mouth.

3   Roll two small balls of black modelling paste and flatten them into discs. Glue the discs onto the back of the ladybird to form the spots (O).

4   Roll two small pieces of white modelling paste into balls and glue them into the eye sockets. Draw a small dot in the centre of each eye using a black edible ink pen.

SPIDER

1   Roll 15g (½oz) of black modelling paste into a ball and flatten it slightly. Roll a small piece of black modelling paste into a pea-sized ball and attach it to one end of the body to form the head.

2   Use the small end of a ball tool to indent the eye sockets. Roll two small pieces of white modelling paste into balls and glue them into the sockets. Draw a small dot in the centre of each eye using a black edible ink pen.

3   Use a no. 00 paintbrush and white edible paint to paint a tuxedo pattern onto the spider's back, as

shown (P). Leave the spider to firm overnight before adding the legs.

4   To make the legs, roll eight small balls of black modelling paste into sausage shapes in the palm of your hand. Bend a right angle in the centre of each leg. Glue four legs along each side of the body, using a Dresden tool to help with positioning.

BEETLE

1   Roll 12g (³/₈oz) of black modelling paste into an ovoid. Use your fingers to pinch out one end of the ovoid to form the head. Use a Dresden tool to draw a deep line down the centre of the body. Repeat to add shallower lines on either side (Q).

2   Use a no. 10 paintbrush to brush Sapphire lustre dust food colour over the beetle's wings (Q). Add a little Ruby lustre dust food colour along the central line.

3   Use a small ball tool to indent the eye sockets. Glue two oval-shaped pieces of white modelling paste into the sockets and add pupils using a black edible ink pen.

4   Knead a pea-sized ball of black modelling paste into the same amount of white modelling paste. Roll the grey modelling paste into a long sausage shape and bend it in half. Glue the strip over the beetle's neck.

5   Repeat step 4 from the Spider instructions to add three legs on each side of the beetle's body.

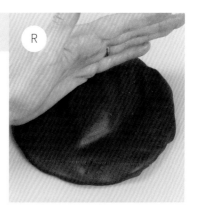

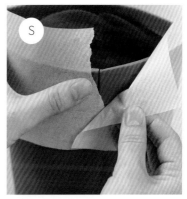

COVERING

1 Use 400g (14oz) of Bridal White sugarpaste to cover the drum (see page 30). Allow the drum to firm overnight.

2 Place the filled cake on the 15cm (6") cake card. Spread a small amount of buttercream over the surface of the 10cm (4") cake card and place it centrally on top of the cake. Use a serrated knife to trim away the sides of the cake at an angle, working from the edge of the 10cm (4") cake card at the top to the edge of the 15cm (6") cake card at the base. Apply a thin crumb coat of buttercream to the side of the cake. Use a side scraper to remove any excess buttercream and create a smooth surface. Chill the cake for approximately five hours.

3 Colour the remaining Bridal White sugarpaste warm orange using Terracotta paste food colour. Use a pastry brush to apply a thin layer of cooled, boiled water to the side of the cake and the 10cm (4") cake card. Roll out the warm orange sugarpaste to a 4mm ($^3/_{16}$") thickness. Lay the sugarpaste over the cake and use your hands to smooth it over the top and down the side. Polish the surface of the sugarpaste with a cake smoother to achieve a neat finish. Trim away the excess sugarpaste with a sharp knife. Set the cake aside to firm for 24 hours.

TOP TIP

If you don't have an airbrush, you can dust the sides of the plant pot using Orange or Nasturtium dust colour and a wide fluffy brush.

POT

1 Once firm, carefully turn the cake upside down so it sits on the 10cm (4") base. Remove the 15cm (6") cake card and spread a layer of buttercream over the top of the cake.

2 Use your hands to shape 280g (9¾oz) of Coco Brown sugarpaste into a 15cm (6") disc. Keep the bulk of the paste in the centre of the disc to create a mound. Use the sides of your hands to create furrows in the mound (R). Lay the sugarpaste disc on top of the cake and use ball tools to indent wells in the surface.

3 Fill the airbrush cup with Bulrush liquid food colour. Holding the tip of the airbrush gun 15cm (6") away from the top of the cake, begin spraying colour over the outer edge and across the grooves in the paste to create shading.

4 Knead ½tsp of CMC into the remaining warm orange sugarpaste. Wrap the paste in cling film and set it aside for two hours.

5 Lightly grease a 46cm (18") strip of baking parchment with white vegetable fat. Roll out the CMC-enhanced warm orange sugarpaste to a 3mm ($^1/_8$") thickness and cut out a 4cm x 46cm (1½" x 18") strip. Lay the strip upside-down onto the greased parchment. Brush the lower 3cm (1$^1/_8$") of the strip with edible glue and use the parchment to lift the strip up to the top edge of the cake, wrapping it around until the ends meet (S). The strip should sit approximately 1cm

(³/₈") above the top of the cake. Use a Dresden tool to add cracks along the top edge of the strip

6   Roll out the remaining CMC-enhanced warm orange sugarpaste into a thin sheet and cut out an oval using the oval cutter. Colour 10g (¼oz) of White SFP using Terracotta paste food colour. Roll out the SFP into a thin sheet and use the alphabet and number cutters to cut out your chosen name and number. Use edible glue to fix the letters in place on the oval. Attach the oval plaque to the front of the cake.

7   Fill the airbrush cup with Leaf Green liquid food colour. Hold the tip of the airbrush gun 15cm (6") away from the covered cake drum and pull back the nozzle to release the spray of colour. Starting at the edge of the drum, apply colour in a circular motion, building up more colour at the edge to create a graduated effect. Set the drum aside to dry for 30 minutes.

8   Fill the airbrush cup with Nasturtium liquid food colour. Use the colour to add shading around the base and top of the plant pot, as well as under the rim and plaque (T). Set the pot aside to dry for 30 minutes. Once dry, fix the plant pot in the centre of the covered drum using a little royal icing.

9   Roll 55g (2oz) of Coco Brown sugarpaste into a sausage with tapered ends. Flatten the sausage in the palm of your hand and use edible glue to fix it to the drum in front of the pot, positioning it towards the left side. Use your fingers to stretch and shape the paste around the outer edge (U). Use the remaining sugarpaste to add small patches of mud around the drum.

SPIDER'S WEB

1   Lay a sheet of baking parchment over the template on page 180 and lightly grease the surface with white vegetable fat.

2   Roll 10g (¼oz) of White SFP into a long, thin sausage. Halfway along the sausage, bend the paste to a point. Lay the SFP on top of the greased paper and trim it to fit the template. Roll a second thin sausage of White SFP and attach it between the two halves of the pointed piece (V). Fill in the scalloped lines of the web using more thin sausages of White SFP, following the lines on the template (W).

3   Once the web is complete, place a cake smoother on top and gently push down to ensure all the pieces are fully adhered. Set the web aside to firm for two hours. Once firm, attach the web to the right side of the pot using a little royal icing (X).

MUSHROOMS

1   Roll 8g (¼oz) of white modelling paste into a cylinder then narrow one end slightly (Y). Glue the shape inside the plant pot.

2   To make the cap, shape 15g (½oz) of red modelling paste into a dome. Roll small balls of white modelling paste and glue them over the surface of the dome, pushing them down to flatten them into spots (Z). Glue the cap in place on top of the stalk.

3   Repeat to make and attach a second, slightly smaller mushroom using 5g (<¼oz) of white modelling paste and 10g (¼oz) of red modelling paste.

WORMS

1   Combine 5g (<¼oz) of pink modelling paste with the same amount of white modelling paste. Roll a marble-sized ball of pale pink modelling paste into a 5cm (2") long sausage.

2   Use a Dresden tool to mark lines across the sausage (AA). Gently bend the sausage into an arc and glue it on top of the cake. Repeat this step with the remaining pale pink paste and fix it over the seam on the rim of the plant pot.

FINISHING TOUCHES

1   Roll out the remaining White SFP into a thin sheet and use the plunger cutters to cut out five daisies.

2   Colour a small amount of white modelling paste using Sunflower paste food colour. Roll the Sunflower-coloured paste into small balls and glue one in the centre of each flower. Set the flowers aside to firm in cupped formers for one hour.

3   Colour a small amount of white modelling paste using Leaf Green paste food colour. Roll the leaf-green-coloured paste into small cones and group them together in threes. Glue the tufts of grass around the drum, along with the daisies.

4   Use edible glue to fix the critters in place on the cake.

5   Wrap green ribbon around the edge of the drum and attach it using double-sided tape.

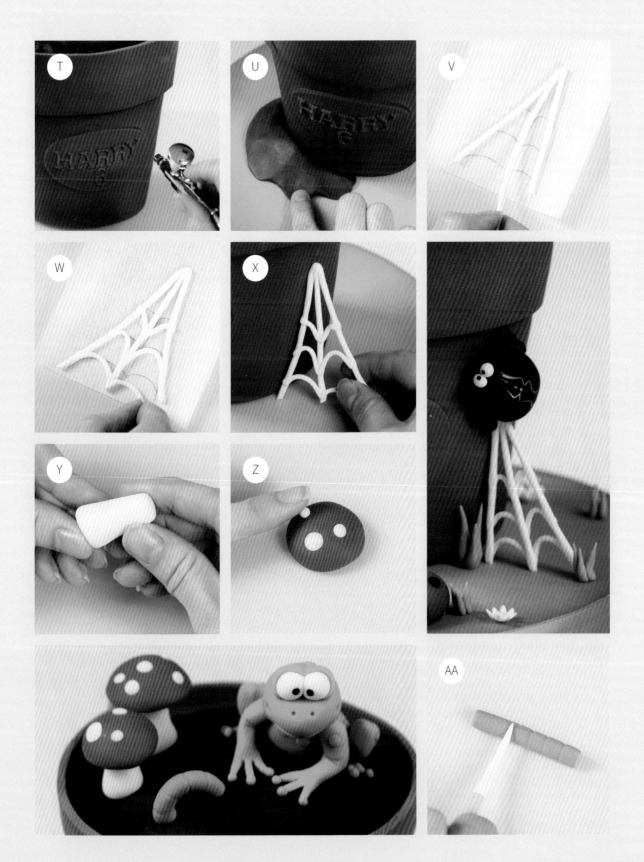

PREHISTORIC PALS

This cake is dino-mite! Learn to make everyone's favourite roar-some dinosaurs, including a diplodocus, a triceratops, a stegosaurus and a T-rex.

DIPLODOCUS

SK HD Sugar Modelling Paste: 5g (<¼oz) Black, 165g (5 7/8oz) Green and 25g (>¾oz) White

CMC cellulose gum

TYRANNOSAURUS REX

SK HD Sugar Modelling Paste: 5g (<¼oz) Black, 85g (2¾oz) Green, 5g (<¼oz) White and 5g (<¼oz) Yellow

SK Sugar Florist Paste (SFP): 85g (2¾oz) White

STEGOSAURUS

SK HD Sugar Modelling Paste: 5g (<¼oz) Black, 10g (¼oz) Blue, 155g (5½oz) Turquoise and 5g (<¼oz) White

TRICERATOPS

SK HD Sugar Modelling Paste: 5g (<¼oz) Black, 150g (5¼oz) Orange, 90g (3oz) White and 5g (<¼oz) Yellow

PREHISTORIC CAKE

SK Professional Paste Food Colour: Marigold

SK Sugarpaste: 500g (1lb 1¾oz) Coco Brown and 800g (1lb 12oz) Palm Green

Round cake drum: 30.5cm (12")

Round, filled, sponge cake, 10cm (4") deep, crumb-coated with buttercream: 15cm (6")

Royal icing: 45g (1½oz) White

CMC cellulose gum

PME Writer Piping Nozzles: nos. 2 and 3

SK Sugar Florist Paste (SFP): 10g (¼oz) White

SK HD Sugar Modelling Paste: 5g (<¼oz) Black, 15g (½oz) Brown and 75g (2½oz) White

DIPLODOCUS

1. Knead a pinch of CMC into 28g (1oz) of green modelling paste. Split the paste into quarters and roll each piece into a squat cylinder. Press a ball tool into the front of the base of each cylinder three times then set the legs aside to firm.

2. Roll 125g (4½oz) of green modelling paste into a ball. Place the sides of your hands on top of the ball and gently rock back and forth to extrude a sausage shape from the centre. Thin the middle of the sausage slightly, leaving a large ball at the top (A). Keep rolling the paste until it reaches a 6cm (2³⁄₈") length. Extrude a cone shape from the other end of the ball to shape the tail then bend it upwards slightly. Redistribute the paste in the centre of the shape so that it flows from the head to the tail (B).

3. For the head, start to pinch and pull a short sausage shape from the centre of the ball. Position the side of your hand over the area where the sausage and ball meet and gently press to flatten. Push a ball tool into the flattened paste on either side of the sausage to create the eye sockets, pushing the ball upwards to create oval-shaped wells (C). Press the rounded handle of a tool into the top of the head, between the eye sockets.

4. Push a wooden skewer from the base of the model up through the neck and into the head for support, leaving 5cm (2") exposed at the base. Place the model on a spare cake dummy while you work.

5. Use your fingers to narrow the middle of the head area, creating a bulbous end. Gently pinch and flatten the base of the sausage into a snout shape. Press a ball tool into the top of the snout to create the nostrils. Roll a small ball of green modelling paste and attach it to the underside of the snout, using a Dresden tool to blend the paste into the neck (D). Elongate the smile using the pointed end of a Dresden tool and finish with a small dot at either end using a mini ball tool.

6. Roll two small pieces of green modelling paste into thin, tapered sausage shapes. Use edible glue to fix one sausage over each nostril (E). Use a scribing tool to mark two horizontal lines over the top of the snout.

7. Fill the eye sockets with pea-sized balls of white modelling paste. Press a ball tool into the base of each eye, towards the inner corners. Fill the resulting wells with small balls of black modelling paste. Add two small balls of white modelling paste to each eye to create highlights.

8. Roll two very fine tapered sausages of black modelling paste and glue one around the top of each eye, guiding them into place with a Dresden tool (F).

9. Knead together 20g (¾oz) of white modelling paste and 10g (¼oz) of green modelling paste. Press variously sized ball tools into the diplodocus' back and neck to create shallow wells. Fill each well with a small ball of the pale green modelling paste.

10. To make the leaf, shape a small ball of pale green modelling paste into a teardrop, flatten it, then use a scribing tool to mark veins in its surface. Glue the leaf just inside the dinosaur's mouth. Add a small sausage of pale green modelling paste to the opposite side of the mouth.

11. For the chest, roll 10g (¼oz) of pale green modelling paste into an elongated cone shape and gently flatten it. Glue the shape to the front of the body and blend the edges with your fingers to create a smooth join. Mark horizontal lines across the chest using a scribing tool.

12. Roll 12 tiny pieces of pale green modelling paste into cone shapes and use edible glue to fix them into the wells created on the legs.

13. Glue the body on top of the legs, pushing the wooden barbecue skewer through the centre.

TYRANNOSAURUS REX

1. Combine 85g (2¾oz) of green modelling paste with the same amount of White SFP. Roll 100g (3½oz) of the pale green paste into a rounded cone shape. Extrude a short, pointed cone from the base of the shape to form the tail. Use the wide end of a Dresden tool to mark horizontal grooves up the back of the body and tail (G). Roll thin, tapered sausage shapes of yellow modelling paste and use them to fill each groove on the back of the model.

2. For the feet, shape 6g (<¼oz) of pale green paste into a cone. Gently pinch the paste at one end of the cone to create a flat foot. Cut into the flattened paste to create three toes (H). Roll the toes between your fingers to round off the cut edges. Add a very small cone of yellow modelling paste to the tip of each toe for the claws. Use a scribing tool to mark creases in the base of the foot. Repeat to create a second foot. Glue one foot to each side of the body.

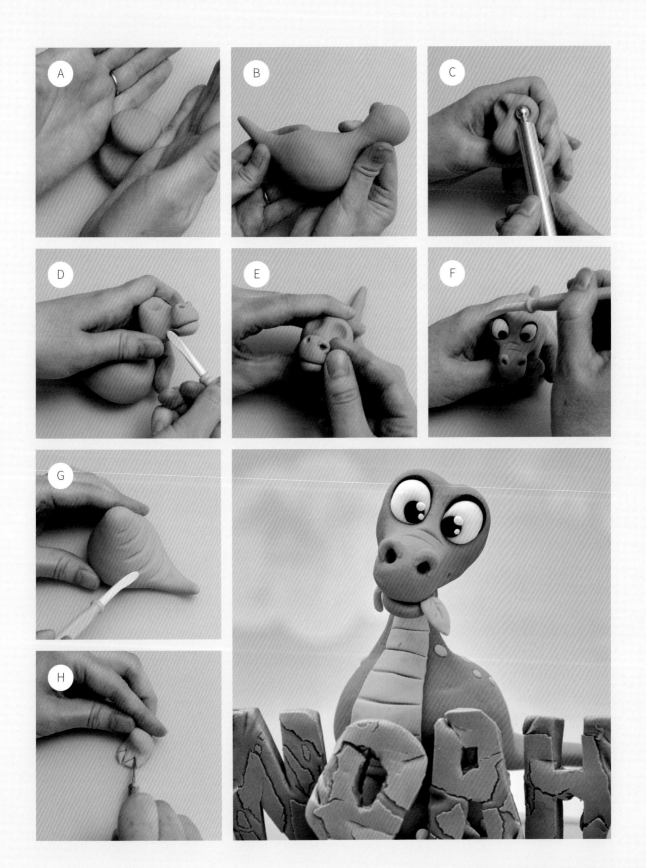

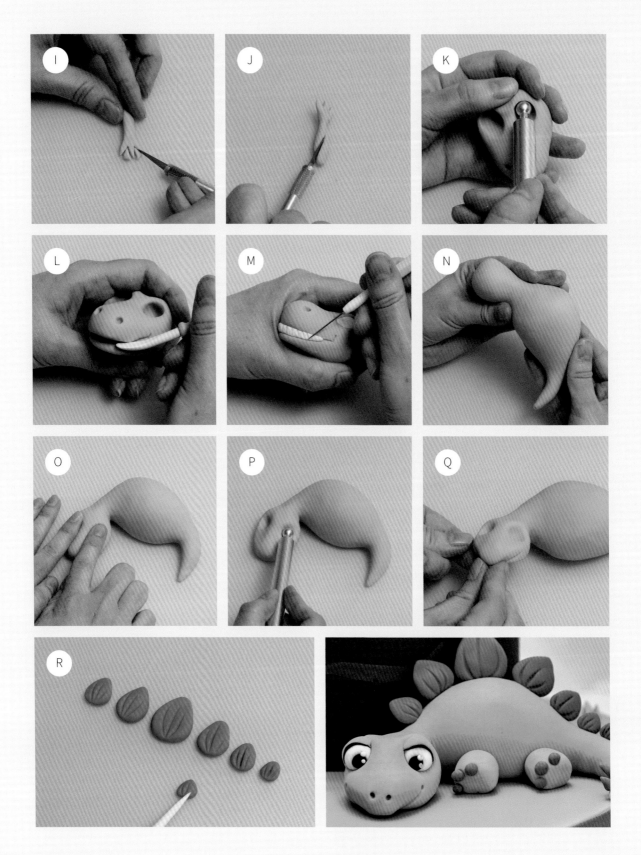

3   For the arms, roll a pea-sized ball of pale green paste into a sausage shape and pinch one end to flatten it. Cut into the flattened area to create three claws (I). Roll them between your fingers to round off the cut edges. Trim the top of the arm horizontally (J). Bend the arm at the elbow and glue it in place on the body, with the hand touching the chest. Repeat to make and attach a second arm.

4   For the head, roll 55g (2oz) of pale green paste into an egg shape. To create the forehead, press the side of your hand over the wide end and push backwards from the thin end of the egg. Push a ball tool into the forehead to create the eye sockets. Push the ball tool upwards and use your fingers to press the paste around the tool to create the exaggerated eyebrow ridge (K). Place your fingertips over the eye sockets and gently press down with your fingers to shape the snout. Round off the tip of the snout then push a mini ball tool into the end to create the nostrils.

5   Use the pointed end of a Dresden tool to draw a mouth then use the wider end of the tool to deepen and widen the smile (L). Use your fingers to shape the top and bottom lips. Press the pointed end of a Dresden tool into the ends of the smile to create dimples. Fill the mouth with a long, tapered sausage of white modelling paste. Use a scribing tool to mark a zig zag in the white paste to represent a set of pointed teeth (M).

6   Fill the eye sockets with balls of white modelling paste, making sure the paste sits inside the sockets by a few millimetres to create a sunken eye effect. Press a mini ball tool into the inner edge of each eye and fill the wells with balls of black modelling paste. Finish with two small balls of white modelling paste for the highlights.

7   Push a wooden barbecue skewer down through the body and trim it so only a small portion remains visible at the neck. Push the head over the exposed skewer and fix it in place with edible glue.

STEGOSAURUS

1   Roll 155g (5¼oz) of turquoise modelling paste into a ball. Roll one end of the ball to a point then gently bend the point back towards the ball; this will form the tail. Extrude a chunky sausage shape from the opposite side of the ball; this will become the head. Thin the paste at the base of the head and bend the top around towards the ball (N).

2   Shape the head area into an egg. Place your fingers on top of the egg, 1cm (³/₈") apart, and gently press down (O). Push a ball tool into the paste where your fingertips were to create the eye sockets (P). Use your fingers to shape the paste around the top of the eyes to create a flat forehead.

3   Draw a mouth in the front of the face using the pointed end of a Dresden tool and finish by pressing a mini ball tool into the ends of the smile to add dimples. Shape the tip of the snout so that it curves downwards into a slight beak shape (Q). Use a mini ball tool to add the nostrils at the front of the snout.

4   Fill the eye sockets with balls of white modelling paste. Press a mini ball tool into the bottom edge of each eye and fill the wells with balls of black modelling paste. Finish with two small balls of white modelling paste for the highlights. Roll two small, tapered sausages of turquoise modelling paste and glue one over the top of each eye. Flatten them to create slightly dozy eyelids then add a very fine, tapered sausage of black modelling paste along the base of each one for the eyelashes.

5   For the feet, repeat step 1 and 12 from the Diplodocus instructions using 5g (<¼oz) of turquoise modelling paste and three small balls of blue modelling paste. Glue the feet to the front side of the stomach.

6   Roll four small cones of blue modelling paste and glue them to the tip of the tail. Split the remaining blue modelling paste into seven balls, one extra-large, two large, two medium and two small. Flatten each ball and shape them into teardrops. Use the pointed end of a Dresden tool to mark three lines in the surface of each teardrop, running from the wide end to the pointed end (R). Glue the plates along the stegosaurus' spine in the following order: medium, large, extra-large, large, medium, small and small.

TOP TIP

You can swap the fine line of Black modelling paste around the top of the eyes with a fine piped line of Black royal icing.

TRICERATOPS

1 Combine 150g (5¼oz) of orange
modelling paste and 75g (2½oz) of
white modelling paste. Roll 140g (5oz)
of the pale orange modelling paste into
a ball. Extrude a short cone from one
end of the ball to form the tail. Carefully
elongate the rest of the ball to lengthen
the body. Use variously sized ball tools
to make shallow wells in the back of the
body then fill the wells with small balls of
yellow modelling paste (S).

2 Roll 5g (<¼oz) of pale orange
modelling paste into a squat
cylinder. Use a mini ball tool to make
three indentations along the bottom
edge. Fill the wells with small balls
of yellow modelling paste. Repeat to
create three more legs. Glue the legs
around the edge of the body.

3 For the head, roll 40g (1½oz) of
pale orange modelling paste into
a ball. Place the side of your hand over
the centre of the ball and gently rock
it back and forth to create a shallow
groove (T). Shape the chin into a
slight point then gently bend the tip
downwards into a beak shape (U). Place
your thumbs over the shallow groove,
leaving a 1cm (³⁄₈") gap between them,
and gently push down to shape the
face. Push a ball tool into the paste
where your fingertips were to create the
eye sockets.

4 Draw a mouth in the front of the
face using the pointed end of a
Dresden tool (V). Press a mini ball tool
into either end of the mouth to create
dimples. Use a scribing tool to mark
three horizontal lines across the bridge
of the nose.

5 Roll two small balls of pale orange
modelling paste and attach them

to the top of the snout. Press a mini
ball tool into the centre of each ball to
create the nostrils (W).

6 Fill the eye sockets with balls of
white modelling paste. Press a
mini ball tool into the bottom edge of
each eye (X). Fill the wells with balls of
black modelling paste then finish with
two small balls of white modelling paste
for the highlights. Roll two very fine,
tapered sausages of black modelling
paste and glue one around the top
edge of each eye, using the Dresden
tool to help guide them into place (Y).

7 To make the horns, roll three
medium and two small cones of
white modelling paste. Glue the two
small cones to either side of the face,
at the outside edges of the mouth.
Attach one medium cone shape to the
centre of the front of the snout and the
remaining two on top of the head. Roll
five very fine sausage shapes of pale

orange modelling paste and glue one
around the base of each cone, using
a Dresden tool to guide them into
place (Z). Push a cocktail stick into the
triceratops' neck, leaving a small area
exposed, then push the head down
onto the stick and fix it in place with
edible glue (AA).

8 To create the triceratops' bony
frill, roll 25g (>¾oz) of pale
orange paste into a short, tapered
sausage shape. Use your hands to
flatten the sausage until the paste is
long enough to wrap around the back
of the head (AB). Use the pointed end
of a Dresden tool to mark six lines in
the surface of the frill, radiating out
from the centre (AC). Glue the frill
around the back of the head (AD). Roll
six tiny balls of white modelling paste
into ovoids and attach one to the end
of each line in the paste.

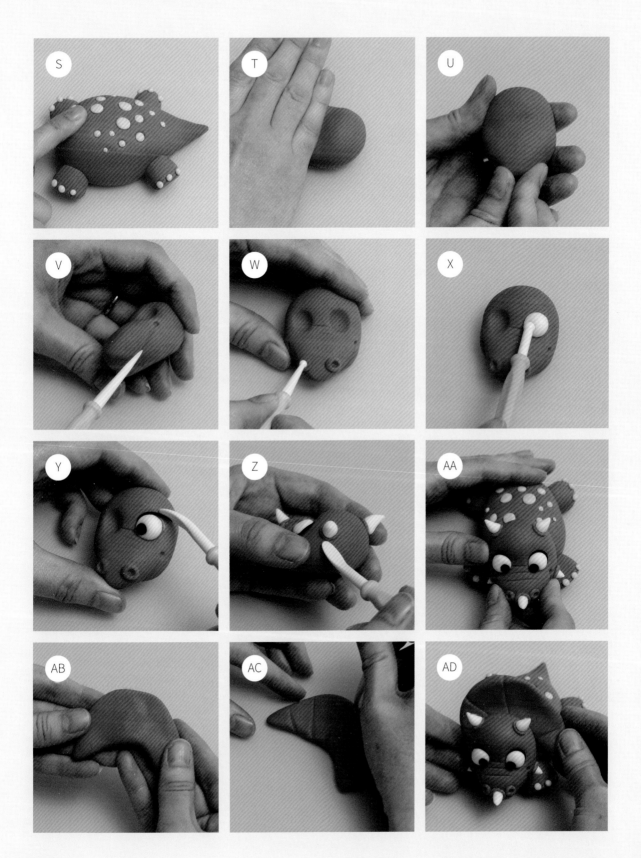

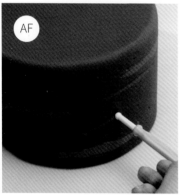

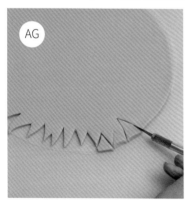

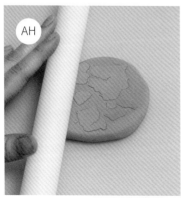

COVERING

1   Knead a little Marigold paste food colour into the Palm Green sugarpaste to create a warm green tone and use it to cover the cake drum (see page 30).

2   Use the Coco Brown sugarpaste to cover the crumb-coated cake (see page 28).

3   Shape 15g (½oz) of brown modelling paste into seven balls of various sizes. Roll each ball into a sausage with tapered ends. Paint a tiny amount of glue in horizontal wavy lines around the side of the cake and glue a sausage on top of each one. Use a smoother to flatten the sausages into the side of the cake (AE).

4   Use a ball tool to impress bone shapes into the side of the cake (AF). Using less pressure, add indents all over the side of the cake using ball tools of various sizes. Set the cake and drum aside to firm for 24 hours.

DECORATION

1   Spread 15g (½oz) of royal icing towards the back of the covered drum and place the cake on top.

2   Place the no. 2 and no. 3 piping nozzles inside piping bags and divide the remaining royal icing between them. Pipe royal icing into the bone-shaped indents on the side of the cake. Use a clean, slightly damp paintbrush to remove any peaks or tails from the piped icing.

3   Knead a large pinch of CMC into the remaining warm-green-coloured sugarpaste. Roll the paste out to a 3mm (⅛") thickness and cut out a 25.5cm (10") disc. Lightly grease a 25.5cm (10") round piece of a baking paper with white vegetable fat. Lay the disc of sugarpaste upside down on the paper. Use a craft knife to cut away irregular triangular shapes from around the edge of the disc (AG).

4   Brush edible glue over the top of the cake then lift the disc, using the baking paper as a support, and attach it over the glued area. Smooth the surface of the sugarpaste then leave it to firm for 24 hours.

LETTERING

1   Combine 8g (¼oz) of White SFP with 2g (<¼oz) of black modelling paste. Roll out the grey paste into a thin sheet and allow to dry.

2   Combine 75g (2½oz) of white modelling paste with 5g (<¼oz) of black modelling paste. Roll the grey modelling paste out to a 2cm (¾") thickness. Glue the dried sheet of grey paste on top of the modelling paste then roll it out to a 1cm (⅜") thickness; the SFP will crack as you roll (AH).

3   Use a craft knife to roughly cut out your chosen letters in a thick, blocky font. Leave the cut marks and don't try to make the letters too symmetrical.

4 Use a Dresden tool and a scribing
tool to texture the surface of the
paste. Leave to firm for one hour before
gluing the letters on top of the cake.

FINISHING TOUCHES

1 Roll 18 small cones of pale green
modelling paste. Fix the cones
into groups of three and glue them
around the cake and drum to form tufts
of grass.

2 Wrap green ribbon around the
edge of the drum and fix it in place
with double-sided tape.

3 Use edible glue to fix the
diplodocus on top of the
cake, behind the lettering. Glue the
tyrannosaurus rex to the front of the
drum, positioning it in front of the middle
of the cake. Glue the stegosaurus to the
right of the tyrannosaurus rex and the
triceratops to its left.

TOP TIP

Create a volcano by covering a
cone of RKT (Rice Krispie Treats) or
Polystyrene in Brown sugarpaste and
adding texture lines with the dresden
tool. Add elongated cones of Red
and Orange modelling paste from
the top dribbling down the sides.

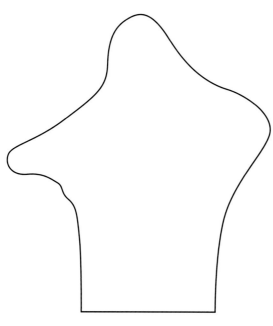

PARTY PUPPIES

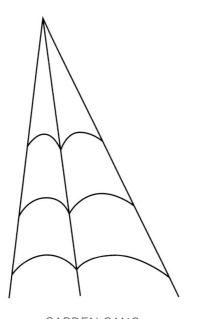

GARDEN GANG

CONVERSION CHART

The conversions are approximate but the difference between an exact and an approximate conversion will not affect your cooking results. Try not to mix metric and imperial measures in one recipe; stick to one system or the other.

Oven Temperatures

Temperatures refer to conventional ovens. For fan-assisted ovens, reduce the temperature by 20°.

°C	°F	GAS MARK
100	200	low
110	225	¼
120	250	½
140	275	1
150	300	2
160	325	3
180	350	4
190	375	5
200	400	6
220	425	7
230	450	8
250	475	9

Liquid Measurements

METRIC	IMPERIAL	US CUPS
30ml	1fl oz	$\frac{1}{8}$ cup
60ml	2fl oz	$\frac{1}{4}$ cup
90ml	3fl oz	$\frac{3}{8}$ cup
120ml	4fl oz	$\frac{1}{2}$ cup
140ml	5fl oz	$\frac{2}{3}$ cup
170ml	6fl oz	$\frac{3}{4}$ cup
200ml	7fl oz	$\frac{7}{8}$ cup
230ml	8fl oz	1 cup
260ml	9fl oz	$1\frac{1}{8}$ cups
290ml	10fl oz (½ pint)	$1\frac{1}{4}$ cups
500ml	17½fl oz	2 cups
600ml	20fl oz (1 pint)	$2\frac{1}{2}$ cups
1 litre	1¾ pints	4 cups

Dry Measurements

METRIC	IMPERIAL
15g	½oz
30g	1oz
60g	2oz
90g	3oz
115g	4oz (¼lb)
140g	5oz
170g	6oz
200g	7oz
225g	8oz (½lb)
255g	9oz
285g	10oz
310g	11oz
340g	12oz (¾lb)
370g	13oz
400g	14oz
425g	15oz
450g	16oz (1lb)
680g	24oz (1½lb)

Cake/cake board sizes

METRIC	IMPERIAL
10cm	4"
12.5cm	5"
15cm	6"
18cm	7"
20.5cm	8"
23cm	9"
25.5cm	10"
28cm	11"
30.5cm	12"
33cm	13"
35.5cm	14"

Check out some of Vicky's other whimsical creations that make up her impressive sugarcraft portfolio.

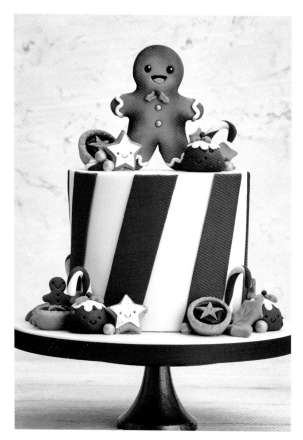

SQUIRES KITCHEN, UK

The Packhouse,
Blackmoor Estate,
Blackmoor,
Liss,
Hampshire
GU33 6BS
+44 (0) 330 223 4466
squires-shop.com

SQUIRES KITCHEN
INTERNATIONAL SCHOOL, UK

The Grange
Hones Yard
Farnham
Surrey
GU9 8BB
+44 (0) 330 223 4466
squires-school.co.uk

OTHER BOOKS FROM B. DUTTON PUBLISHING

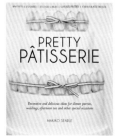
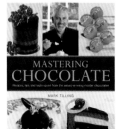
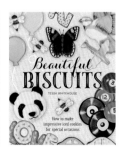

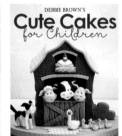